ISBN: 0-9772923-0-4
ISBN 13: 978-0-9772923-0-1

Y0-AGL-378

You can visit us online at:

www.GrowingWithGrammar.com

Printed in the United States of America.

Ver. 2.0.0-3

Preface

For many years, I have been aware that educators around the world are in need of a thorough grammar program that can be used by anyone regardless of their background or beliefs. *Growing With Grammar* was developed to fill that need in the education community.

We have designed this thorough program to be user-friendly for both teacher and student by separating the subject matter into two books, the Student Manual and the Student Workbook (which includes a separate Answer Key). The Student Manual contains the learning portion of the subject matter and the Student Workbook contains the hands-on portion which reinforces the lessons taught in the Student Manual. If desired, independent learners can work alone by utilizing the Student Manual and Student Workbook since the Answer Key is separate. To support each concept learned in the Student Manual there is a corresponding workbook lesson. Review questions are integrated within each workbook lesson to constantly provide reinforcement of previous lessons learned. In addition, there are separate review lessons at the end of each chapter. There are 105 lessons in the Level 3 program and 5 review lessons, for a total of 110 lessons.

Also, we have selected spiral binding for our books to ensure that they lie flat when open. The spiral binding on the workbook is at the top of the page to provide equal, unobstructed access for both right and left handed students.

Thank you for choosing *Growing With Grammar*, we look forward to the opportunity to provide you with the best tools possible to educate your children.

Chapter 1 - Growing with Sentences

Chapter 2 - Growing with Nouns and Pronouns

Chapter 3 - Growing with Verbs

Chapter 4 - Growing with Adjectives and Adverbs

Chapter 5 - Growing with Words and Punctuation

Chapter 1

Growing with Sentences

1.1 Sentences

A sentence is a group of words that expresses a complete thought.   A sentence contains a **subject** and a **predicate**.

The **subject** names the person, place, or thing the sentence is about.

Kristin rode a horse.

What or who is this sentence about? The subject of this sentence is **Kristin**.

The **predicate** tells what the subject is or does.

Kristin **rode a horse**.

What did the subject do? The predicate of this sentence is **rode a horse**.

All sentences begin with a **capital letter** and end with a **punctuation mark**.

In the following examples, each group of words is a complete sentence.

Dad made pizza.

My sister walked to the store.

A tree was planted.

They stopped at a park.

The apple is juicy.

Serena likes math.

The door was open.

Bruce owns a mouse.

Jay had a birthday party.

1.2 Fragments

Not every group of words forms a sentence. **If a group of words does not express a complete thought, it is a fragment.**

Notice in the following examples that each fragment is only part of a complete sentence.

Wrote a letter.

Swayed in the wind.

Was happy.

Grazed in the field.

Across the road I saw.

Who wrote a letter? What swayed in the wind? Who was happy? What grazed in the field? Across the road I saw what? These groups of words do not give the reader enough information.

   Fragments can be turned into sentences by adding
the missing words needed to express a complete
thought.

Wrote a letter. → **She** wrote a letter.

Was happy. → **Jill** was happy.

Grazed in the field. → **The cows** grazed in the field.

Across the road I saw. → Across the road I saw **Mom.**

Swayed in the wind. → **The tree** swayed in the wind.

1.3 Run-On Sentences/Compound Sentences

A **run-on sentence** is actually two or more sentences that run together without correct punctuation to separate or join them. One way to fix a run-on sentence is to separate it into two sentences.

Incorrect: Joey found a quarter he will put it in his bank.

This example can be written correctly by making two separate sentences.

Correct: Joey found a quarter. He will put it in his bank.

Look at these examples.

Incorrect: It is cold outside do you have mittens?
Correct: It is cold outside. Do you have mittens?

Incorrect: Last week we sailed this week we will ski.
Correct: Last week we sailed. This week we will ski.

Another way to correct run-on sentences is to turn them into **compound sentences**. A **compound sentence** is two or more simple sentences that are related in meaning and joined by words like **and**, **but**, or **or**. These words are called **coordinating conjunctions**. **Conjunctions** are words that connect parts of sentences. A **comma** is placed before these joining words.

run-on sentence: Al has a dollar he will put it in his bank.

compound sentence: Al has a dollar**, and** he will put it in his bank.

run-on sentence: Last week we skied this week we sailed.

compound sentence: Last week we skied**, but** this week we sailed.

Also, combining short sentences helps to avoid boring or choppy writing.

choppy sentences: Courtney can multiply. She can divide.

combined sentence: Courtney can multiply, **and** she can divide.

1.4 Complex Sentences

A **simple sentence** has a **subject** and a **verb** and expresses **a complete thought**. Simple sentences are also called **independent clauses**.

<u>Bradley shut the windows</u>.
↑
independent clause

As we learned in lesson **1.3**, a **simple sentence** **(independent clause)** can be joined with another simple sentence **(independent clause)** to form a **compound sentence**. The **clauses** of a compound sentence are joined by a **comma** and a **coordinating conjunction**.

<u>Bradley shut the windows</u>, *and* <u>he left the house</u>.
↑   ↑   ↑
independent clause   conjunction independent clause

A **simple sentence (independent clause)** can also become a **complex sentence** when you add a **dependent clause**. A **dependent clause** has a **subject** and a **verb**, however, it does **not** express a **complete thought**. It **cannot** stand on its own. A **dependent clause** needs an **independent clause**. When you join the two, you have a **complex sentence**.

<u>Bradley shut the windows</u> <u>before he left the house</u>.
↑   ↑
independent clause   dependent clause

Dependent clauses usually begin with a word like **after**, **although**, **before**, **because**, **if**, **since**, **unless**, **until**, **when**, or **while**. These are called **subordinating conjunctions**.

In the previous example, the **dependent clause** begins with the word **before**.

<u>**before**</u> **he left the house**

This clause **cannot** stand on its own, so it's **dependent** on the **independent clause**. The entire sentence is a **complex sentence**.

More examples of **complex sentences**:

<u>The dog barked **when** the man arrived</u>.
       ↑   ↑
independent clause   dependent clause

<u>Mark baked a cake **since** he was hungry</u>.
       ↑   ↑
independent clause   dependent clause

<u>We watched a great move **after** Tom left</u>.
       ↑   ↑
independent clause   dependent clause

<u>Todd slipped on the soap **while** washing the dog</u>.
       ↑   ↑
independent clause   dependent clause

1.5 Statements

There are four kinds of sentences. They are **statements**, **questions**, **commands**, and **exclamations**. Each kind requires a specific ending punctuation.

The first kind of sentence is a **statement**. A **statement** tells something. It gives information and states a fact. A statement begins with a capital letter and ends with a period.

Anthony is eating soup.

The rabbit is brown and white.

The first sentence gives information about what Anthony is eating. The second sentence tells the color of the rabbit. A sentence always expresses a complete thought.

More examples:

Tom wrapped a gift.

The doorbell rang.

My brother is funny.

The puppy chased its tail.

Hayden stayed home.

We walked two miles.

Allison washed the car.

The sky is blue.

Your clothes are wrinkled.

The queen sat on her throne.

1.6 Questions

The second kind of sentence is a **question**. A **question** asks something and requires an answer. A question begins with a capital letter and ends with a question mark.

Is that vegetable soup?

Who kicked the ball?

Both of these sentences ask something specific.

More examples:

What color was the flower?

When did she leave?

What are you studying?

Who won the game?

How many snowballs did you throw?

When is your birthday?

Where is my jacket?

How did you break your glasses?

What did you put on your hamburger?

Are you going skateboarding?

1.7 Commands

The third type of sentence is a **command**. A **command** makes a request or tells you to do something. A command begins with a capital letter and ends with a period, or sometimes can end with an exclamation mark. The subject of a command is always **you**, but it is not always spoken or written in the sentence. We say that the subject **you** is understood.

(You) Hand me a spoon.

You wash your hands.

The subject in the first sentence is **you** even though it isn't stated. In the second sentence, **you** is a part of the command.

More examples:

Get out your history book.

You feed the cat.

Take off your shoes.

Shoot the basket.

You do the laundry.

Have a cookie.

You come here!

Pick up the toys.

Help me pull weeds.

Do your lessons.

1.8 Exclamations

The fourth type of sentence is an **exclamation**. An **exclamation** expresses strong feeling or emotion. An exclamation begins with a capital letter and ends with an exclamation mark.

That is delicious!

You are strong!

Both sentences express strong or sudden emotion.

More examples:

Look out for that car!

We won the game!

Don't quit!

My picture is ruined!

I don't believe it!

Don't step on my toe!

There's a snake!

I am so excited!

That music is too loud!

Watch out!

1.9 Yes/No Questions

There are many different types of questions. One is
a **Yes/No** question. The answer to the question is **Yes**
or **No**.

Do you live in New York?

Is it cold outside?

They can be answered with a simple **Yes** or **No** or
with a longer answer beginning with one of these
words. You must use a comma after yes or no.

Do you live in New York?

No, I live in New Jersey.

Is it cold outside?

Yes, it is cold.

Will you visit us next summer?

Yes, I will.

Do you like to play basketball?

Yes, I love playing basketball.

Are you seven years old?

No, I am eight years old.

1.10 Wh- Questions

   Wh- questions are answered with more than a yes or no. These types of questions are useful for finding out information.   **Wh-questions** start with words such as **what, when, where, which, who, whose, why,** or **how.**

What is used when you are asking for information about something.

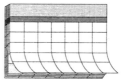

>   **What** is today's date?
>   **What** is your name?

When is used to ask about time.

>   **When** is the big race?
>   **When** will you be done with your work?

Where is used to ask about location.

>   **Where** did you put your jacket?
>   **Where** do you live?

Which is used when there are several things from which to choose.

>   **Which** picture do you like best?
>   **Which** shoes are you going to wear to the ball?

Who is used to ask about a person's identity.

>**Who** ate the last cookie?

>**Who** sings that song?

Whose is used to ask about possession.

>**Whose** toy is this?

>**Whose** car is that?

Why is used to ask for a reason.

>**Why** didn't you do your chores?

>**Why** did you park your car in the road?

How is used to ask for an explanation of the method in which something is done.

>**How** do you build a birdhouse?

>**How** was your vacation?

1.11 Alphabetical Order

When words are in **alphabetical order**, they are arranged in order according to the alphabet. Sometimes this is called **ABC order**.

To alphabetize words, put words that begin with **A** before words that begin with **B**. Put words that begin with **B** before words that begin with **C**, and so on.

Examples:

apple	**h**ike	**r**abbit
banana	**j**ump	**s**nake
carrot	**l**eap	**t**urtle
egg	**m**arch	**v**ulture
grape	**p**lay	**z**ebra

These words are in alphabetical order.

Often, words start with the same letters. When the first two letters of words are alike, the words are listed according to the third letter. When the first three letters of words are alike, the words are alphabetized by the fourth letter, and so on.

Examples:

bat	draw	theft
bee	dresser	their
big	drink	there
book	drop	these
bug	dry	they

1.12 Using the Dictionary

Learning to use the **dictionary** is an important skill. The dictionary shows how to spell words and how to say them. It also tells the meanings of the words. The words in the dictionary are called **entry words**.

 **Kitten** (kit-en) a young cat.

The letters in parentheses tell you how to pronounce the entry word **kitten**. There is sometimes more than one pronunciation for a word.

Ketchup (kech'*u*p, kach'*u*p) a thick spicy sauce made with tomatoes.

The group of words after the parentheses is the definition, which tells what the word means.

The first step to finding a word in the dictionary is to find the section of the dictionary in which the word will be found. Words that start with **A, B, C, D, E, F,** or **G,** are found near the **front** part of the dictionary. Words that start with **H, I, J, K, L, M, N, O,** or **P,** are found

near the **middle** of the dictionary. Words that start with
Q, R, S, T, U, V, W, X, Y, or **Z,** are found near the **back**
part of the dictionary.

After the correct section of the dictionary is found, the
next step in locating a word is to look at the **guide**
words. The guide words are the words at the top of
each page. The guide word on the left tells you the first
word on the page. The guide word on the right tells
you the last word on the page. All other words on that
page occur alphabetically between the two guide
words.

kilowatt   **kneel**

The word **kitten** can be found on a dictionary page with
the guide words **kilowatt** and **kneel.**

The last step to finding a word is to look at the **entry**
words. The **entry words** are listed in the dictionary in
alphabetical order.

1.13 The Two Parts of a Sentence

A sentence expresses a complete thought. Every sentence consists of two parts: the **subject** and the **predicate.**

The **complete subject** contains all the words that tell **who** or **what** the sentence is about.

My cousin Gina | played the piano.

Who is the sentence about? The complete subject is **My cousin Gina**.

The **complete predicate** contains all the words that tell what the subject **is** or **does.**

My cousin Gina | **played the piano.**

What did Gina do? The complete predicate is **played the piano**.

More examples divided into subject and predicate:

My father | cooked dinner.

    ↑   ↑

complete subject   complete predicate

My best friend | sang a song.

    ↑   ↑

complete subject   complete predicate

The little boy | laughed out loud.

    ↑   ↑

complete subject   complete predicate

Black ants | crawled in the grass.

    ↑   ↑

complete subject   complete predicate

My mother | mowed the lawn.

    ↑   ↑

complete subject   complete predicate

The angry bees | stung the boys.

    ↑   ↑

complete subject   complete predicate

1.14 Simple Subjects and Predicates

The **simple subject** is the main noun or pronoun that names the subject. It is usually one word. It tells **who** or **what** the sentence is about.

Example:	Many dogs run through the field.
complete subject:	Many dogs
simple subject:	dogs

The **simple predicate** is the verb in the complete predicate that tells what the subject **does** or **is**.

Example:	Susan ran in a race.
complete predicate:	ran in a race
simple predicate:	ran

A sentence **diagram** is a simple way of dividing a sentence into its basic parts. Many students find that they can understand a sentence better when they use a diagram.

In a diagram, the subject and predicate are placed on a horizontal line with the simple subject on the left, the simple predicate on the right. A short vertical line divides the subject area from the predicate area.

Mimi baked bread.

Mimi	baked

Jacob washed the car.

Jacob	washed

Harry helped Fred.

Harry	helped

Mom ate spinach.

Mom	ate

1.15 Compound Subjects

You have learned how to identify the simple subject of a sentence. Some sentences, however, have two or more subjects. This is called a **compound subject**.

Example: **Miguel** and **Ron** played.

Who played? **Miguel** and **Ron** tell who, and they are the compound subject of the sentence.

Example: **Ants** and **spiders** crawl.

What crawls? **Ants** and **spiders** tell what, and they are the compound subject of the sentence.

Sentences with a **compound subject** are diagrammed like this:

Miguel and **Ron** played.

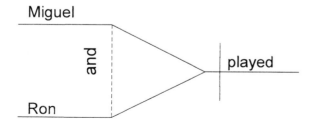

Ants and **spiders** crawl.

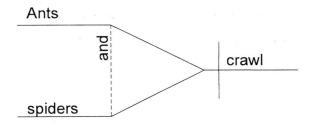

Kim and **Diane** worked.

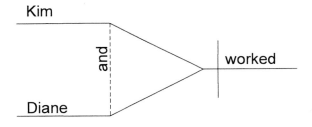

Birds and **bees** fly.

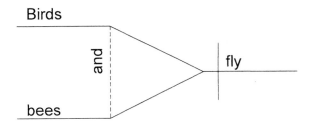

1.16 Compound Predicates

Just as a sentence can have a compound subject, it can also have a **compound predicate**. A compound predicate is two or more verbs in the sentence that tell what the subject is doing.

Example: Children **hopped** and **skipped**.

What did the children do? **Hopped** and **skipped** tells what they did, and they are the compound predicate of the sentence.

Example: Ducks **paddled** and **splashed**.

What did the ducks do? **Paddled** and **splashed** tells what they did, and they are the compound predicate of the sentence.

Sentences with a **compound predicate** are diagrammed like this.

Children **hopped** and **skipped**.

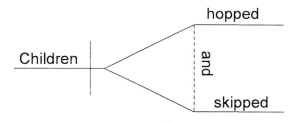

Ducks **paddled** and **splashed**.

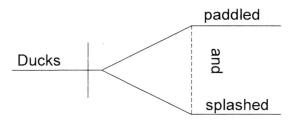

They **laughed** and **smiled**.

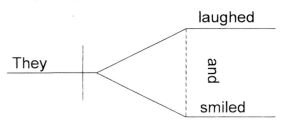

1.17 Subjects and Predicates in Questions

In most sentences, the subject comes before the verb. However, in some sentences, such as questions or asking sentences, the verb comes **before** the subject.

Example: Do birds sing?

To find the subject in questions, rephrase the question as a statement. This will place the subject before the verb.

Example: Birds do sing.

The simple subject is **birds**. The simple predicate is **do sing**. The verb can consist of more than one word. This is called a verb phrase.

The sentence **Do birds sing?** is diagrammed like this.

birds	Do sing

Below are more examples of questions and their
diagrams.

Did he learn?

he	Did learn

Are people leaving?

people	Are leaving

Can we play?

we	Can play

Is Barbara moving?

Barbara	Is moving

Does Sean swim?

Sean	Does swim

1.18 Subjects and Predicates in Commands

In a request or command, the **subject** of a sentence is usually not stated. The subject of a command is understood to be **you** because the person speaking is giving you an order or asking you for a favor. The word **you** is not usually spoken or written. The subject is **you** (understood).

(**You**) Jump!

(**You**) Come here.

The missing subject, **you**, is diagrammed by placing the word **you** in parentheses.

Clean the dishes.

(you)	Clean

Open your book.

(you)	Open

Sometimes a command will include **you** and a name. Then the command has a compound subject. This time **you** is stated and not understood.

You and Skylar clean.

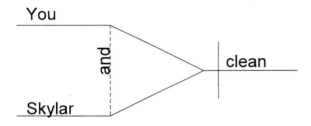

You and Michael listen.

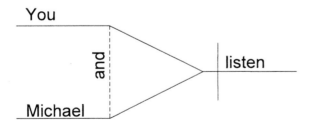

1.19 Direct and Indirect Quotations

Direct quotations are another person's exact words.

When you are including a direct quotation in your writing, you should place quotation marks before and after the exact words of the speaker. A comma is placed between the speaker's words and the other words in the sentence.

Examples: Samantha said, "I love horses."

"That apple is juicy," said Anthony.

The first word in the quotation is capitalized. End punctuation goes inside the quotation marks when the quote is at the end of the sentence.

Examples: Joshua said, "I spilled my lemonade."

"I am going to the store," said Aunt Tina.

Question marks and exclamation marks that are part of the quotation are placed inside the closing quotation marks.

Examples: Elijah asked, "Where are you going**?**"

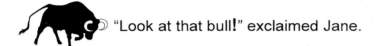 "Look at that bull**!**" exclaimed Jane.

"Go**!**" yelled Percy.

"Are you going home**?**" asked Jenny.

Indirect quotations are not exact words but summaries or shortened versions of another person's words. Do not use quotation marks for indirect quotations.

Examples: Michael said that he won the race.

Molly said that she is nine years old.

Claude said that the train was coming.

Caitlin said that she would be here soon.

1.20 Paragraphs

It is important to know how to write a **paragraph**. A paragraph is a series of sentences about one idea. The first sentence should be a **topic sentence**, and it should be indented. An indented sentence is one that is set in about half an inch from the left margin.

A **topic sentence** states the main idea of the paragraph. The other sentences describe and give more detail about the main idea.

Correct example:

> **I made spaghetti for my family**. First I boiled the noodles. Then I drained the noodles. Next I added the sauce. The spaghetti was finished.

In the paragraph above, the sentence *I made spaghetti for my family* is the topic sentence. The other sentences give more detail about it.

It is important to remember that there should be no unrelated sentences in your paragraph.

Incorrect example:

> I made spaghetti for my family. First I boiled the noodles. **My brother loves basketball**. Then I drained the noodles. Next I added the sauce. The spaghetti was finished.

The sentence *My brother loves basketball* is not related to the topic sentence. It really does not belong in this paragraph.

The sentences of a paragraph should be put together in a way that makes sense to the reader.

Incorrect example:

> Then I drained the noodles. The spaghetti was finished. First I boiled the noodles. I made spaghetti for my family. Next I added the sauce.

These sentences are not in the correct order. The paragraph does not make sense.

1.21 Writing a Paragraph

There are **three steps** in writing a paragraph. The **first step** is to plan what the paragraph will be about. It is important to make sure the chosen topic is not too big. For example, the topic "My Family" might be too big. However, you could choose one person in your family to write about. You could also choose one characteristic about your family as your topic. After the topic is chosen, write down as many ideas about it as you can.

Example:

Topic → things I like about my dad

Ideas: He is funniest person I know.

He tells goofy jokes.

He is nice to everybody.

He plays basketball with me.

He lets me win.

When I need to talk to someone, he listens to me.

He loves me.

My sister is five years old.

The **next step** is to write the paragraph. Choose a topic sentence and make sure it states the main idea for the paragraph.

Example: There are many things I like about my dad.

Look at your list of ideas. Does each of the ideas tell about the main topic? If there are any that do not, then you should not use them. The sentence **My sister is five years old** does not have anything to do with the topic.

Put the ideas into sentences. Look at the order of the sentences and find a way that sounds best.

Example:

There are many things I like about my dad. He is nice to everybody. He tells goofy jokes. He is the funniest person I know.   He plays basketball with me and lets me win. When I need to talk to someone, he listens to me. The thing I like best about my dad is that he loves me.

The **final step** is to correct any mistakes in your paragraph. Check to make sure you indented the first line, you started each sentence with a capital letter, you ended each sentence with the correct punctuation, and that you spelled each word correctly.

Chapter 1 Review

Sentences: A **sentence** is a group of words that expresses a complete thought.   A sentence contains a subject and a predicate.   All sentences begin with a capital letter and end with a punctuation mark.

Fragments: If a group of words does not express a complete thought, it is a **fragment**.

Run-On Sentences: Two sentences that run together without correct punctuation to separate or join them are called **run-on sentences**.

Compound Sentences: A **compound sentence** is two or more simple sentences that are related in meaning and joined by words like **and**, **but**, or **or**. These words are called **coordinating conjunctions**. **Conjunctions** are words that connect parts of sentences. A **comma** is placed before these joining words.

Complex Sentences: A **simple sentence (independent clause)** can also become a **complex sentence** when you add a **dependent clause**. A **dependent clause** has a **subject** and a **verb**, however, it does **not** express a **complete thought**. It **cannot** stand on its own. A **dependent clause** needs an **independent clause**. When you join the two, you have a **complex sentence**.

Dependent clauses usually begin with a word like **after**, **although**, **before**, **because**, **if**, **since**, **unless**, **until**, **when**, or **while**. These are called **subordinating conjunctions**.

<u>Statements</u>: A **statement** is a sentence that tells something. Statements begin with a capital letter and end with a period.

<u>Questions</u>: A **question** is a sentence that asks something and requires an answer. Questions begin with a capital letter and end with a question mark.

<u>Commands</u>: A **command** is a sentence that commands you to do something. Commands begin with a capital letter and end with a period. The subject of a command is always **you**, but it is not always written in the sentence. We then say that the subject **you** is understood.

<u>Exclamations</u>: An **exclamation** is a sentence that expresses strong feeling or emotion. Exclamations begin with a capital letter and end with an exclamation mark.

<u>Alphabetical Order</u>: When words are in **alphabetical order** this means they are arranged in order according to the alphabet. Sometimes this is called **ABC order**.

Sentence Diagram: A **diagram** is a picture that shows the basic parts of a sentence. These parts are placed on a horizontal line with the simple subject on the left and the simple predicate on the right. A short vertical line divides them.

Examples:

Jacob washed the car.

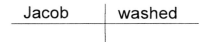

Miguel and Ron played.

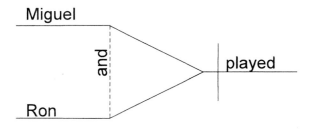

Children hopped and skipped.

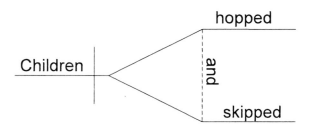

Subjects and Predicates in Questions: To find the subject in questions, rephrase the question as a statement. This will place the subject before the verb.

Subjects and Predicates in Commands: The subject of a command is understood to be **you** because the person speaking is giving you an order or asking you for a favor. The word **you** is not usually spoken or written. The subject is **you** (understood).

Direct and Indirect Quotations: **Direct quotations** are another person's exact words. When you are including a direct quotation in your writing, you should place quotation marks before and after the exact words of the speaker. The first word in the quotation is capitalized.

Indirect quotations are not exact words but summaries of another person's words. Do not use quotation marks for indirect quotations.

48

Chapter 2

Growing with Nouns and Pronouns

2.1 Nouns

Nouns are naming words. A **noun** is the name of a **person**, **place**, or **thing.**

Person	Place	Thing
nurse	library	stone
boy	city	tree
girl	pond	box
mayor	garden	paper
author	forest	computer
friend	beach	dog
doctor	store	basketball
neighbor	country	book
sister	lake	shoe
father	state	can
uncle	restaurant	doll
grandmother	mountain	blanket

Most sentences have a noun as the subject.

The **cow** is brown.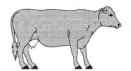

The **library** is closed.

My **basketball** is flat.

Cow, **library**, and **basketball** are nouns. They are the subjects of these sentences.

Nouns are divided into two groups: **common nouns** and **proper nouns**.

A **common noun** names any person, place, or thing. Common nouns are usually not capitalized unless they begin a sentence or are part of a title.

2.2 Proper Nouns/Concrete and Abstract Nouns

A **proper noun** is the specific name of a **person**, **place**, or **thing**. Begin the first word and every other important word in a **proper noun** with a **capital letter**.

Common noun	Proper noun
river	Nile River
city	Indianapolis
novelist	Jane Austen
holiday	Labor Day
building	Chrysler Building
state	California
boy	Joshua Baker
inventor	Thomas Edison
school	Harvard University
month	June
day	Friday
dog	Spot
man	Bob Cohen
superhero	Spiderman
country	Australia
street	Main Street
zoo	Brookfield Zoo
president	John F. Kennedy
doctor	Dr. Lansky

Concrete nouns are nouns that can be **seen, heard, smelled, tasted,** or **felt.**

music	friend	chair	bread
photograph	onion	sister	radio
flower	perfume	flute	sandpaper

These examples are **concrete nouns.** Most nouns are concrete nouns.

Concrete nouns can also be **proper nouns.**

Nile River   Aunt Mary   Eiffel Tower

Abstract nouns are nouns that **cannot** be **seen, heard, smelled, tasted,** or **felt.** They represent **ideas, emotions,** or **qualities.**

love	peace	fear	wealth
fun	justice	calm	belief
freedom	friendship	luck	anger
beauty	kindness	generosity	idea
honor	courage	goodness	success
wisdom	trust	truth	bravery

If you cannot see the noun, it is most likely an **abstract noun.**

2.3 Capitalizing Names, Initials, and Titles

A person's **name** is a proper noun. Each part of a person's **name** including the **first, middle,** and **last** names should be capitalized.

Incorrect: james davis   *Correct*: James Davis

Incorrect: robert potter   *Correct*: Robert Potter

Incorrect: hannah jacobs   *Correct*: Hannah Jacobs

Incorrect: tami ann chen   *Correct*: Tami Ann Chen

Capitalize **initials** that take the place of names. Initials should also be followed by a period.

Incorrect: g. patel   *Correct*: G. Patel

Incorrect: edward j. cohen   *Correct*: Edward J. Cohen

Incorrect: k. s. jackson   *Correct*: K. S. Jackson

Incorrect: n. turner   *Correct*: N. Turner

Capitalize **titles** that are used before a person's name.

Mr. Edward J. Cohen   **A**unt Nadia

Mrs. Hannah Jacobson   **U**ncle Joe

Miss Tamara Ann Chen   **D**octor Baker

Professor Black   **P**resident Washington

2.4 Capitalizing the Names of Places and Organizations

Capitalize the specific names of schools, clubs, organizations, libraries, and hospitals.

Schools: Harvard University
                        Tremont High School

Clubs: American Kennel Club
                        Girls Club of America

Organizations: National Basketball Association
                        American Red Cross

Libraries: National Agricultural Library
                        New York Public Library

Hospitals: Columbia Animal Hospital
                        Methodist Hospital

Capitalize the names of stores, restaurants, other businesses, particular buildings, or monuments.

Stores: **W**algreens **D**rugstore
                             Academy **B**ookstore

Restaurants: **R**alph's **S**teakhouse
                             Arturo's **I**talian **R**estaurant

Businesses: **F**ord **M**otor **C**ompany
                             Kraft **F**oods

Buildings: **C**hrysler **B**uilding
                             Eiffel **T**ower

Monuments: **W**ashington **M**onument
                             Statue of **L**iberty

2.5 Capitalizing Geographical Names

Most geographical names are proper nouns and should be capitalized.

Towns and Cities:	**Los Angeles**
	Rome
States and Provinces:	**New Jersey**
	North Dakota
	Alberta
Countries:	**United States of America**
	Italy
	Mexico
Continents:	**North America**
	Africa
	Europe
Islands:	**Hawaiian Islands**
	Galapagos Islands
Mountains:	**Great Smoky Mountains**
	Mount Everest

Bodies of Water:

Nile River
Atlantic Ocean
Lake Erie

Roads and Highways:

Gilbert Street
U.S. Highway 90
Aslan Avenue

Deserts:

Mojave Desert
Arabian Desert

Parks:

Yosemite National Park
Everglades National Park

2.6 Capitalizing Days

Capitalize the days of the week, months of the year, and holidays.

Days of the Week: **M**onday

Wednesday

Months of the Year: **A**pril

September

Holidays: **T**hanksgiving

Father's **D**ay

Fourth of **J**uly

The names of the seasons are common nouns and do **not** begin with a capital letter.

summer   fall / autumn   winter   spring

Capitalize the names of languages, nationalities, religions, and religious terms.

Languages: Italian

Swedish

Chinese

Nationalities: Canadian

Australian

Irish

Religions: Judaism

Christianity

Hinduism

Religious Terms: Buddha

God

Koran

2.7 Singular and Plural Nouns

Nouns can be **singular** or **plural**. The **singular** form of a noun indicates **just one** person, place, or thing. The **plural** form of a noun indicates **more than one** person, place, or thing.

Most nouns can be made plural by just adding **-s** to the end of a word.

tree → tree**s**   horse → horse**s**

bay → bay**s**   boat → boat**s**

clock → clock**s**   bed → bed**s**

If the noun ends with **s; ch, sh, x,** or **z,** add **-es** to make it a plural noun.

kiss → kiss**es**   dish → dish**es**

box → box**es**   stitch → stitch**es**

buzz → buzz**es**   peach → peach**es**

Some nouns end with **f** or **fe**. To make these plural, change the **f** to **v** and add **-es**.

knife → kni**ves**   life → li**ves**

hoof → hoo**ves**   shelf → shel**ves**

wolf → wol**ves**   loaf → loa**ves**

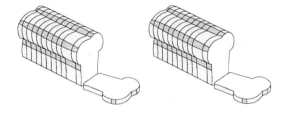

2.8 More Singular and Plural Nouns

There are other ways to form **plural nouns**.

When a noun ends with **y** after a **vowel,** the plural is made by adding **-s**.

guy → guy**s**   monkey → monkey**s**

toy → toy**s**   day → day**s**

donkey → donkey**s**   bay → bay**s**

boy → boy**s**   alley → alley**s**

turkey → turkey**s**   highway → highway**s**

valley → valley**s**   essay → essay**s**

Some nouns end with a consonant letter and **y**. Change the **y** to **i** and add **-es** to form the plural.

body → bod**ies**   cherry → cherr**ies**

berry → berr**ies**   pony → pon**ies**

fly → fl**ies**   family → famil**ies**

sky → sk**ies**   baby → bab**ies**

country → countr**ies**   copy → cop**ies**

penny → penn**ies**   lady → lad**ies**

2.9 Irregular Plural Nouns

Some plural nouns have special spellings. These are called **irregular plural nouns**.

more than one **foot** → **feet**

more than one **mouse** → **mice**

The spelling of the nouns **foot** and **mouse** are changed to form the plurals **feet** and **mice**.

More examples:

man → men	gentleman → gentlemen
tooth → teeth	woman → women
ox → oxen	child → children
person → people	policeman → policemen
goose → geese	fireman → firemen

Some nouns do not change when they are used as plural.

one swine → four swine

one deer → three deer

one sheep → many sheep

one fish → two fish

one bison → some bison

one trout → many trout

one salmon → six salmon

one moose → two moose

2.10 Possessive Nouns

A **possessive noun** is a word that shows ownership.
Possessive nouns are formed by adding an **apostrophe**
and an **-s ('s)**.

the dress of the girl → the **girl's** dress

a badge of a policeman → a **policeman's** badge

A possessive noun tells **whose**.

Whose dress is it? It is the **girl's** dress.

Whose badge is it? It is a **policeman's** badge.

The words **girl's** and **policeman's** are possessive nouns.
The possessive form of a noun shows that the person or
thing named possesses something.

More examples:

the dog that belongs to Todd → **Todd's** dog

the toy that is owned by Dora → **Dora's** toy

the whiskers of the cat → the **cat's** whiskers

the books that are owned by Dad → **Dad's** books

the mother of John → **John's** mother

a hat that belongs to Lee → **Lee's** hat

a waiting room of a doctor → a **doctor's** waiting room

the ship of the pirate → the **pirate's** ship

the idea of the boy → the **boy's** idea

the eggs that belong to the duck → the **duck's** eggs

2.11 Series of Nouns

Use **commas** to separate three or more nouns in a series. The number of commas that should be used in a series is **one less than the number of nouns,** because you put a comma after each noun except for the last noun in the series. If you have three nouns, you should use two commas. If you have four nouns, you should use three commas.

Joel, Doug, and **Michael** came to my birthday party.

Amy loves **dogs, cats, birds,** and **horses**.

In the first sentence, there are **three nouns** so only **two commas** are required. In the second sentence, there are **four nouns** so **three commas** are required.

More examples:

4 nouns and 3 commas

We went to the **library, supermarket, mall,** and **toy store** today.

3 nouns and 2 commas

Amy brought **sandwiches, drinks,** and **pie** to the picnic.

5 nouns and 4 commas

Serena, Caitlin, Sami, Kayla, and **Grace** are in my ballet class.

4 nouns and 3 commas

Emma planted **onions, carrots, beans,** and **tomatoes** in the garden.

3 nouns and 2 commas

Dashiell's favorite subjects are **history, science,** and **math**.

5 nouns and 4 commas

The clown's shoes were **red, green, blue, yellow,** and **orange**.

2.12 Compound Nouns

A **compound noun** is made up of two or more words that are used together to form a single noun.   Compound nouns normally have two parts. The two parts can be written as one word.

police + man → policeman

motor + cycle → motorcycle

The words **police** and **man** are two separate words, but when they are joined together they form the new word **policeman**.   The words **motor** and **cycle** are also two separate words, but they become the word **motorcycle** when joined together.

mail + box → mailbox

seat + belt → seatbelt

light + house → lighthouse

basket + ball → basketball

bed + room → bedroom

key + board → keyboard

drug + store → drugstore

book + case → bookcase

flower + pot → flowerpot

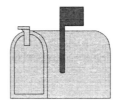

Some compound nouns can be written as two separate words.

fountain + pen → fountain pen

tree + trunk → tree trunk

The words **fountain** and **pen** are two separate words, but when they are used together they form the new word **fountain pen**. The words **tree** and **trunk** are also two separate words, but they become the new word **tree trunk** when used together.

onion + skin → onion skin

post + office → post office

fire + drill → fire drill

ticket + agent → ticket agent

fish + tank → fish tank

ice + cream → ice cream

meat + loaf → meat loaf

tennis + ball → tennis ball

guest + house → guest house

bubble + bath → bubble bath

You should check a dictionary if you are unsure how to write a particular compound noun.

2.13 Nouns of Direct Address

A **noun of direct address** is the name of someone being spoken to directly.

Place a comma after the noun of direct address when it is used **at the beginning of a sentence.**

John, let's play soccer.

Rebecca, may I ask you a question?

Maggie, here's your scarf.

Mom, may I have a cookie?

Brett, hand me that eraser.

Place a comma before the noun of direct address when it is used **at the end of a sentence.**

Let's go swimming, **Shamar**.

I'm going home with you, **Grandma**.

Come here, **Marco**.

That's correct, **Gabriella**.

Would you like to come with us, **Henry**?

Place a comma before and after the noun of direct address when it is used **in the middle of the sentence.** Sometimes this is called a **comma sandwich**.

Yes, **Trevan**, it is your turn.

To be honest, **Brenna**, I'm not sure.

No, **Chantal**, I didn't have time to finish it.

I think, **Tina**, that we should go outside.

Yes, **Kylan**, I would love to help you.

2.14 Pronouns

A **pronoun** is a word that takes the place of a noun. Common pronouns include **I, you, he, she, it, we, they, me, her, him, us,** and **them**.

Zoe is a great gymnast. → **She** is a great gymnast.

The **cups** and **dishes** are clean. → **They** are clean.

In the first sentence, the pronoun **she** replaces **Zoe**. In the second sentence, the pronoun **they** replaces **cups** and **dishes**.

More examples:

Bethany and Emily are talking. → **They** are talking.

Dad makes breakfast. → **He** makes breakfast.

Dad read **Lou and me** a story. → Dad read **us** a story.

My brother saw a **tiger**. → My brother saw **it**.

When using pronouns, it is not necessary to keep repeating nouns.

Sue was going to let **Sue's** sister borrow **Sue's** dress.

↓

Sue was going to let **her** sister borrow **her** dress.

Using the pronoun **her** in place of the noun **Sue** improves the sound of the sentence.

More examples:

Karla ate **Karla's** cake. → Karla ate **her** cake.

Jose framed a picture that **Jose** drew. → Jose framed a picture that **he** drew.

Di's dad made **Di's** bed. → Di's dad made **her** bed.

2.15 Subject Pronouns

Pronouns that are used as the subjects of sentences are **subject pronouns.** The pronouns **I, you, he, she, it, we,** and **they** are used in the subject.

Serena loves to eat cake. → **She** loves to eat cake.

Tom and **Sam** ran home. → **They** ran home.

In the first example, the pronoun **she** takes the place of **Serena**. **She** is the subject. In the second example, the pronoun **they** takes the place of **Tom and Sam**.

More examples:

The **waves** are high. → **They** are high.

Hector will be here. → **He** will be here.

Tamy and **Tony** ate lunch. → **They** ate lunch.

The **parade** begins at noon. → **It** begins at noon.

The **books** fell on the floor. → **They** fell on the floor.

The **library** is new. → **It** is new.

Becky is tall. → **She** is tall.

The **dog** ate the bone. → **It** ate the bone.

Sonya and I ate popcorn. → **We** ate popcorn.

The **spider** ate the fly. → **It** ate the fly.

2.16 Object Pronouns

Pronouns that are used in the predicates of sentences are **object pronouns**. The pronouns **me, you, him, her, it, us,** and **them** are used in the predicate.

Jason does not like **pasta**. → Jason does not like **it**.

Max gave his pen to **Joe**. → Max gave his pen to **him**.

In the first example, the pronoun **it** takes the place of **pasta** in the predicate. In the second example, the pronoun **him** takes the place of **Joe**.

More examples:

The dog licked **Roy** and **Mark**. → The dog licked **them**.

Did John break the **telephone**? → Did John break **it**?

The girls waved at **Penny**. → The girls waved at **her**.

Take a picture of **Erik**. → Take a picture of **him**.

The costume is for **Arden**. → The costume is for **her**.

The pie was for **Michael**. → The pie was for **him**.

I gave the ring to **Joy.** → I gave the ring to **you.**

They cancelled the **game**. → They cancelled **it**.

I told jokes to **Zach** and **Mandy**. → I told jokes to **them**.

The bee stung **Sloane** and **me.** → The bee stung **us**.

2.17 Possessive Pronouns

Possessive pronouns show **whose** something is and never need apostrophes. The pronouns **my**, **mine, your, yours, her, hers, his, its, our, ours, their**, and **theirs** are possessive pronouns.

Dean's dog howls. → **His** dog howls.

Where is the **cat's** toy? → Where is **its** toy?

In the first example, the possessive pronoun **his** stands for the possessive noun **Dean's**. In the second example, the possessive pronoun **its** stands for the possessive noun **cat's**.

More examples:
The pumpkin belongs to **Brian**. → The pumpkin is **his**.

The coat belongs to **Cora**. → The coat is **hers**.

The green car belongs to **us**. → The green car is **ours**.

This book belongs to **you**. → This book is **yours**.

Lisa's snake is brown. → **Her** snake is brown.

This picture belongs to **me**. → This is **my** picture.

That truck belongs to **them**. → That is **their** truck.

The dress **you** own is lovely. → **Your** dress is lovely.

The tree that belongs to **us** is tall. → **Our** tree is tall.

The bike belongs to **me**. → The bike is **mine**.

2.18 I or Me?

Sometimes you must decide between **I** or **me** as a pronoun in a sentence. The easiest way to do this is to think of your sentence as two sentences and ask yourself what pronoun you would use if the noun were not there. When you add the noun, don't change the form of the pronoun.

Examples: Molly and (**I** or **me**) went to the library.

Separate into
two sentences: Molly went to the library.

I went to the library.

-or-

Me went to the library.

The pronoun **I** is the correct pronoun for this sentence.

The answer: Molly and **I** went to the library.

Name yourself last when you are talking about another person and yourself.

Father gave Nicholas and (**I** or **me**) a ride.

*Separate into
two sentences:*   Father gave Nicholas a ride.

Father gave **me** a ride.

The answer: Father gave Nicholas and **me** a ride.

Brady and (**I** or **me**) saw a camel.

*Separate into
two sentences:*   Brady saw a camel.

I saw a camel.

The answer: Brady and **I** saw a camel.

Mom read a story to Henry and (**I** or **me**).

*Separate into
two sentences:*   Mom read a story to Henry.

Mom read a story to **me**.

The answer: Mom read a story to Henry and **me**.

2.19 We or Us?

Sometimes you must decide between **we** or **us** as a pronoun in a sentence. Think of your sentence as two sentences and ask yourself what pronoun you would use if the noun were not there. When you add the noun don't change the form of the pronoun.

Examples: Grandpa and (**we** or **us**) walked.

Separate into
two sentences: Grandpa walked.

              We walked.
                -or-
              Us walked.

The pronoun **we** is the correct pronoun for this sentence.

The answer: Grandpa and **we** walked.

Remember to name yourself last when you are talking about another person and yourself.

The cat followed Peter and (**we** or **us**).

Separate into
two sentences: The cat followed Peter.

The cat followed **us**.

The answer: The cat followed Peter and **us**.

Mom and (**we** or **us**) went to the library.

Separate into
two sentences: Mom went to the library.

We went to the library.

The answer: Mom and **we** went to the library.

The police officer helped Stephen and (**we or us**).

Separate into
two sentences: The police officer helped Stephen.

The police officer helped **us**.

The answer: The police officer helped Stephen and **us**.

2.20 Clear Pronoun References

As we learned before, a **pronoun** is a word used for a noun or the name of a person or object. The specific noun or name it substitutes should be used at least once before you use a pronoun.   Otherwise, the sentence is confusing.

Unclear: **She** told a joke.   (Who told a joke?)
Clear: **Lilly** told a joke.

Unclear: **It** flew high. (What flew high?)
Clear: The **hawk** flew high.

A pronoun must make clear which noun is being replaced.

Unclear: Jacob smiled proudly at Jim as **he** received the award.   (Who received the award?)

Clear: As Jim received the award, Jacob smiled proudly at **him**.

Unclear: Abby and Lauren flew kites. **Her** kite fell.

(Whose kite fell?)

Clear: Abby and Lauren flew kites. **Lauren's** kite fell.

When you use a pronoun, be sure to drop the noun it is replacing to avoid redundancy.

Incorrect: The toy **it** is expensive.

Correct: It is expensive.

Incorrect: Kristin **she** loves flowers.

Correct: She loves flowers.

Incorrect: The boy and girl **they** ate breakfast.

Correct: They ate breakfast.

2.21 Personal Pronouns

Personal pronouns can be divided into three groups: **first person, second person,** and **third person.**

Personal pronouns of the **first person** refer to the person **who** is speaking. This includes the pronouns **I, we, me, us, my, mine, our,** and **ours.**

I love warm weather.

My mother will take **me** to **my** recital.

Are **we** driving to **our** grandmother's house?

Personal pronouns of the **second person** refer to the person **to whom** we are speaking. This includes the pronouns **you, your,** and **yours.**

You are a great basketball player.

Is that **your** pencil?

The green coat is **yours.**

Personal pronouns of the **third person** refer to the person **about whom** we are speaking. This includes the pronouns **he, she, it, him, her, his, hers, its, they, them, their,** and **theirs.**

She wrote a letter to **him**.

Is **he their** grandfather?

That globe is **hers**.

2.22 This, That, These, and Those

This, that, these, and **those** are **words** that are used to point out specific persons, places, or things.

That is my picture.

These are beautiful pictures.

When referring to a singular person, place, or thing use **this** or **that**.

This is my piano.

That is Greg's piano.

When referring to a plural person, place, or thing use **these** or **those**.

These are our flowers.

Those are Diana's flowers.

This and **these** refer to nouns that are close to the speaker.

This is my toy.

These are your toys.

Those and **that** refer to nouns that are at a greater distance from the speaker.

That is our horse over there.

Those are beautiful horses in the next field.

Chapter 2 Review

Nouns: A **noun** is the name of a **person, place**, or **thing**. Every sentence must have a noun as its subject.

Concrete Nouns: **Concrete nouns** are nouns that can be **seen, heard, smelled, tasted**, or **felt**.

Abstract Nouns: **Abstract nouns** are nouns that **cannot** be **seen, heard, smelled, tasted**, or **felt**. They represent **ideas, emotions**, or **qualities**.

Common Nouns: A **common noun** names any **person, place**, or **thing**. Common nouns are usually not capitalized unless they begin a sentence or are part of a title.

Proper Nouns: A **proper noun** is the specific name of a **person, place**, or **thing**. Begin the first word and every other important word in a proper noun with a capital letter.

Concrete nouns: Concrete nouns are nouns that can be **seen, heard, smelled, tasted**, or **felt**.

Abstract nouns: Abstract nouns are nouns that **cannot** be **seen, heard, smelled, tasted**, or **felt**. They represent **ideas, emotions**, or **qualities**.

Rules for capitalizing:

–Each part of a person's name including the first, middle, and last names should be capitalized.

–Initials that take the place of names.

–Titles that are used before a person's name.

–The specific names of schools, clubs, organizations, libraries, and hospitals.

 –The names of stores, restaurants, other businesses, particular buildings, or monuments.

–Most geographical names.

–The days of the week, months of the year, and holidays.

 –The names of languages, nationalities, religions, and religious terms.

Singular and Plural Nouns:

–Most nouns can be made plural by just adding **-s.**

–If the noun ends with **s, ch, sh, x,** or **z,** add **-es** to make it a plural noun.

–There are some nouns that end with **f** or **fe.** To make these plural, change the **f** to **v** and add **-es.**

–When a noun ends with **y** after a **vowel**, the plural is made by adding **-s.**

 –Some nouns end with a consonant letter and **y.** Change the **y** to **i** and add **-es** to form the plural.

Possessive Nouns: A **possessive noun** is a word that shows ownership. Possessive nouns are formed by adding an **apostrophe** and an **-s ('s)**.

Series of Nouns: Use **commas** to separate three or more nouns in a series. The number of commas that should be used in a series is **one less than the number of nouns**.

Compound Noun: A **compound noun** is made up of two or more words that are used together to form a single noun.

Noun of Direct Address: A **noun of direct address** is the name of someone being spoken to directly.
-Place a comma after the person's name when it is used **at the beginning of a sentence.**
-Place a comma before the person's name when it is used **at the end of a sentence.**
-Place a comma before and after the person's name when it is used **in the middle of the sentence.**

Pronoun: A **pronoun** is a word that takes the place of a noun. Common pronouns include **I, you, he, she, it, we, they, me, her, him, us,** and **them**. A pronoun must make clear which noun is being replaced.

Possessive Pronouns: **Possessive pronouns** show **whose** something is and never need apostrophes. The pronouns **my, mine, your, yours, her, hers, his, its, our, ours, their,** and **theirs** are possessive pronouns.

Pronouns This, That, These, and Those: **This** and **that** are used with singular nouns. **These** and **those** are used with plural nouns. **This** and **these** tell about things nearby. **That** and **those** tell about things far away.

Chapter 3

Growing with Verbs

3.1 Action Verbs

An **action verb** is a word that tells what the subject is doing. The most important part of the predicate is the verb.

Leah **throws** the ball.

Luke **bakes** a cake.

The **action verb** tells what **action** someone or something is performing. In the first sentence, the action verb is **throws.** It tells what **Leah** is doing. In the second sentence, the action verb is **bakes.** It tells what **Luke** is doing.

More examples:

Bob **laughs**.	Balls **bounce**.
Caleb **reads**.	Flora **writes.**
Birds **sing**.	Ashley **swims**.
Jesse **falls**.	Jon **speaks**.
Spiders **spin**.	Madison **lifts**.

Flowers **grow**.   Angela **draws**.

Butterflies **fly**.   Dogs **chase**.

Sheila **shouts**.   Bears **roar**.

3.2 Action Verbs We Cannot See

Most **action verbs** talk about actions we can see. We can see someone or something baking or throwing. Action verbs may also represent actions that take place but cannot easily be seen.

That **smells** fishy.

I **think** that is a great idea.

The words **smells** and **think** are action verbs but they describe actions that cannot be seen.

More examples:

Jake **likes** his wagon.

He **decided** to stay home.

That **sounds** like Mary's voice.

I **wonder** if it will rain.

She **wants** to win.

I **like** chocolate cake.

He **knew** the answer.

We **have** a brand new car.

I **remember** this song.

Bob **prefers** this color.

3.3 Present Tense

Verbs tell if something has already happened, if it will happen later, or if it is happening now. Verbs that show what is happening now are said to be in the **present tense.**

The dog **barks**.

The bees **buzz**.

The verbs **barks** and **buzz** are in the **present tense.** They tell what the **dog** and the **bees** are doing right now.

If the subject is **it, she**, or **he**, then add **-s** to the verb to show present tense.

It **feels** soft.   She **sees** me.   He **needs** a bath.

Do not use an **-s** with subjects that are **I, you**, or are **plural**.

I **like** chocolate.   You **look** lost.   They **walk** fast.

If the verb ends with a **consonant letter** followed by a **y**, then change the **y** to i and add **-es**.

Helen **hurries** home.   The truck **carries** fruit.

More examples:

The helicopter **flies**.

The lion **roars**.

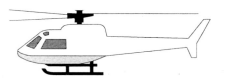

Terry **irons**.

The cats **eat**.

We **watch**.

The children **play**.

Tim **cries**.

The cars **stop**.

3.4 Future Tense

Verbs that tell about something happening in the future are called **future tense**.   The future tense is formed by using **will** or **shall** before the verb.

She **will show** you her new hat tomorrow.

I **shall come** home in an hour.

The verbs **will show** and **shall come** tell us about something that will happen some time later. **Will** and **shall** are used before verbs to show future tense.

Shall and **will** are used with the pronouns **I** and **we**. For all other nouns and pronouns, only **will** is used.

More examples:

I **shall fly** a kite tomorrow.

He **will look** at the painting later.

Henry **will sweep** the floor.

They **will enjoy** the play.

We **shall go** to the movies.

We **will run** in the race.

The lion **will feed** her cubs.

Alexa **will drive** a car today.

I **shall talk** to my mother.

The store **will open** soon.

3.5 Past Tense

Verbs that tell what has already happened are called **past tense**.

The cat **jumped**.

The children **explored**.

The verbs **jumped** and **explored** are in the past tense. These verbs tell what the **cat** and **children** already did.

More examples:

The flowers **bloomed**.

Dad **worked** all day.

Sam **pulled** weeds.

Mom **laughed** at my joke.

Marlee **studied** history.

The dog **jumped** in the air.

Joey **looked** for insects.

The frog **hopped** into the pond.

The children **talked** quietly.

Patrick **carried** the box.

3.6 Forming Past Tense Verbs

To form the **past tense** of most **verbs**, add **-ed** to the verb. Other past tense verbs follow different rules.

Some verbs end with **e**. Drop the **e** and add **-ed**.

taste → tast**ed**   bake → bak**ed**

name → nam**ed**   arrive → arriv**ed**

like → lik**ed**   race → rac**ed**

Some verbs end with a **consonant letter** and a **y**. Change the **y** to **i** and add **-ed**.

study → stud**ied**   hurry → hurr**ied**

marry → marr**ied**   cry → cr**ied**

bury → bur**ied**   worry → worr**ied**

Some verbs end with **a single vowel** followed by **a single consonant**. **Double the final consonant** and add **-ed**.

grab → grab**bed**   stub → stub**bed**

skip → skip**ped**   beg → beg**ged**

fan → fan**ned**   stop → stop**ped**

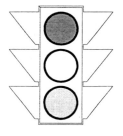

3.7 Irregular Verbs

Verbs in the past tense tell about an action that has already happened. It is easy to form the past tense of most verbs by adding **-ed**.

However, some verbs are **irregular verbs**. You do **not** add **-ed** to form the past tense of an irregular verb. Instead, you must change the spelling of these verbs to form the past tense, and it is usually best to memorize these forms.

Examples:

      begin → began   throw → threw

More examples:

teach → taught   catch → caught

say → said   build → built

buy → bought   win → won

stand → stood   hold → held

keep → kept

lose → lost

bring → brought

sleep → slept

spend → spent

fight → fought

go → went

eat → ate

sing → sang

pay → paid

leave → left

come → came

send → sent

sit → sat

get → got

wind → wound

see → saw

run → ran

grow → grew

know → knew

3.8 Subject - Verb Agreement

The **subject** and **verb** of a sentence must agree in number. If the **subject** is **singular**, the **verb** must be **singular**. If the **subject** is **plural**, the **verb** must be **plural**, too.

Verbs in the present tense frequently end with **-s**. We call this the **-s form** of the verb. If the subject of the sentence is **singular** and means **he, she,** or **it**, use the **-s form** of the verb.

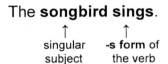

The **songbird sings**.

singular   -s **form** of
subject   the verb

If the subject of the sentence is **plural** or means **we** or **they**, use the **plain form** of the verb (without an **-s**).

The **songbirds sing**.

plural   **plain form** of
subject   the verb

More examples:

Kayla loves ballet.

The **girls love** ballet.

The **boy plays** ball.

The **boys play** ball.

Nina likes eggs.

The **girls like** eggs.

A **bear eats** meat.

Many **bears eat** meat.

Grandpa makes fudge.

Many **people make** fudge.

Jacob reads well.

The **girls read** well.

One **flower blooms**.

Ten **flowers bloom**.

The **bell rings** loudly.

The **bells ring** loudly.

Jack looks handsome.

The **boys look** handsome.

The **kitten cleans**.

The **kittens clean**.

3.9 Pronoun – Verb Agreement

A **subject pronoun** and its verb must match, too.

Use the **-s** form of the verb with the pronouns **he, she,** or **it**.

She measures the room.

↑   ↑
singular   -s form of
subject   the verb

If the subject of a sentence is **I, you, we,** or **they**, use the **plain form** of the verb (without an **-s**).

They measure the room.

↑   ↑
plural   plain form of
subject   the verb

More examples:

He speaks softly.

You speak softly.

She needs a pencil.

I need a pencil.

It ran across the street.

We ran across the street.

He combs his hair.

They comb their hair.

She waits for the bus.   **He paints** a picture.

You wait for the bus.   **I paint** a picture.

She sits on the couch.   **It sounds** wonderful.

We sit on the couch.   **You sound** wonderful.

He reads a book.   **It looks** like a big ship.

I read a book.   **They look** like big ships.

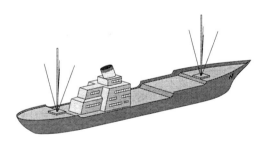

3.10 Linking Verbs

Linking verbs do not show action. They link the subject to a word in the predicate that names or describes it. A **linking verb** shows that something **is, was,** or **will be** something. It is the main verb in the sentence.

Leo **is** the winner.   Ruby **was** happy.

↓   ↓

Leo = winner   Ruby = happy

In the first sentence, the linking verb **is** connects the subject, **Leo**, to additional information about him, that he is the **winner**. In the second sentence, the linking verb **was** connects the subject, **Ruby**, to a description of her, that she was **happy**.

Linking verbs are often forms of the verb **be**. The verb **be** has eight different forms.

am   is   are   was   were   be   being   been

We **were** late.   I **am** eight years old.

The vase **is** cracked.   You **are** smart.

Jordan **was** a waiter.   You **were** funny.

We **are** tired.   Casey **was** in the band.

She **is** a dancer.   They **were** skaters.

3.11 Using the Forms of Be

There are rules for using the verb **be**. It is important to choose the correct form to match the subject of the sentence.

am   is   are   was   were

Use **am** or **was** with the pronoun **I**.

I am a great artist.

I was late.

Use **is** or **was** with the pronouns **she**, **he**, **it**, and **singular** nouns.

The **turtle was** small.

She is my friend.

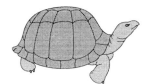

The **door is** open.

The **baby was** hungry.

Kevin is my brother.

Use **are** or **were** with the pronouns **you**, **we**, **they**, and **plural** nouns.

They are volleyball players.

The **children are** sleepy.

You were correct.

We are excited about our vacation.

The **girls were** frightened.

3.12 Helping Verbs

A **verb** that helps another verb is called a **helping verb**. It comes before the main verb to tell about the action.

John **will ride** his scooter.

She **has lost** her tooth.

In the first sentence, the word **will** is a **helping verb** to the main verb **ride**. In the second sentence, **has** is a **helping verb** to the main verb **lost**.

There are **23** helping verbs and they are usually arranged into five different groups.

am	have	do	shall	may
is	has	does	will	might
are	had	did	should	must
was			would	can
were				could
be				
being				
been				

The bells **are ringing**.

Dad **was working** in the yard.

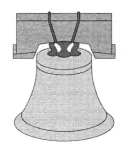

She **is acting** in a play.

Elaine **might tell** us a story.

Andy **has gone** to the store.

Were you **talking** to me?

Does Charles **want** a snack?

I **have written** a poem.

Did you **learn** something new?

   The different forms of **be** are helping verbs only when they are used with another verb. **When a form of be is the only verb, it is the main verb.**

She **is** my mother.   They **are** sisters.

I **am** a dancer.   He **was** early.

3.13 Verb Phrases

A **verb phrase** is a group of words with a main verb plus one or more helping verbs. The main verb is the last word in the verb phrase.

Trudy **is going** home.

I **am writing** a poem.

In these sentences, the verb phrases are **is going** and **am writing**. The main verbs are **going** and **writing**.

More examples:

We **were helping** Vanessa.

You **have been eating** too much.

Betsy **will be leaving** soon.

He **has done** his chores.

You **have been sleeping** all morning.

I **was planting** carrots in the garden.

I **am reading** my book.

Kim **was drinking** pink lemonade.

Carlos **is buying** a new skateboard.

I **had lost** my ring.

3.14 Do, Does, and Did as Action Verbs

Do is an irregular verb that can be used as an **action verb** or a helping verb. **Does** and **did** are forms of the verb **do**.

When used alone **do**, **does**, and **did** are **action verbs** and the main verbs in the sentence.

I **do** my work.

He **does** cartwheels.

You **did** a great job.

Use **do** with **I**, **you, we, they,** or a **plural subject**.

Police officers do important work.

I do the mowing.

You do it alone.

Use **does** with **he**, **she**, **it**, or a **singular subject**.

The girl does a loud cheer.

He does amazing card tricks.

Naomi does a lot of babysitting.

Did is the **past tense** form of the verb **do**.

I did the cooking.

Dana did a great back flip.

He did his chores.

3.15 Do, Does and Did as Helping Verbs

When used with another verb, the verb **do** and its forms **does** and **did** are **helping verbs**.

Pam **did jump** higher than Shayla.

You **do love** to eat chocolate.

He **does care** about his grades.

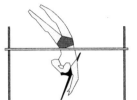

Sarah **did play** beautifully.

I **do know** him.

She **does need** help.

Put **do**, **does**, or **did** before the subject when asking a question.

Did Pam **jump** higher than Shayla?

Do you **love** to eat chocolate?

Does he **care** about his grades?

Did Sarah **play** beautifully?

Do I **know** him?

Does she **need** help?

3.16 Have, Has, and Had as Action Verbs

Have is an irregular verb that can be used as an **action verb** or a helping verb. **Has** and **had** are forms of the verb **have**.

When used alone, **have**, **has**, and **had** are **action verbs** and the main verbs in the sentence.

Use **have** with **I**, **you, we, they,** or a **plural subject**.

The **children have** instruments.

I have an idea.

We have a great family.

Use **has** with **he**, **she**, **it**, or a **singular subject**.

He has a cold.

Zoe has ballet practice.

The **dog has** a bone.

Had is the **past tense** form of the verb **have**.

Suzi had a party.

I had a great day.

We had meatloaf for dinner.

Lane had tickets to the movie.

3.17 Have, Has, and Had as Helping Verbs

When used with another verb, the verb **have** and its forms **has** and **had** are **helping verbs**.

Robert **had closed** the door.

You **have drawn** a picture.

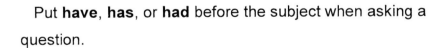

He **has gone** to the pool.

I **have eaten** breakfast.

She **has played** with the puppy.

Hilary **had cleaned** her room.

Put **have, has,** or **had** before the subject when asking a question.

Had Robert **closed** the door?

Have you **drawn** a picture?

Has he **gone** to the pool?

Have I **eaten** breakfast?

Has she **played** with the puppy?

Had Hilary **cleaned** her room?

3.18 Contractions

A **contraction** is a single word made by combining two other words. The words are combined and some letters are dropped. The letters that are dropped are replaced by an apostrophe.

Examples:

have not → haven't   was not → wasn't

did not → didn't   is not → isn't

are not → aren't   could not → couldn't

In these examples, the apostrophe takes the place of the letter **o.**

In other contractions, more than one letter is dropped.

Examples:

I will → I'll   they will → they'll

he would → he'd   cannot → can't

she will → she'll   I would → I'd

More examples:

were not → weren't   you are → you're

I am → I'm   do not → don't

he is → he's   we will → we'll

we have → we've   it is → it's

you have → you've   will not → won't

there is → there's   what is → what's

let us → let's   must not → mustn't

who is → who's   they have→ they've

it will → it'll   that is → that's

I have → I've   you will → you'll

does not → doesn't   has not → hasn't

she is → she's   would not → wouldn't

should not → shouldn't   had not → hadn't

3.19 Not Is Not a Verb

Although the word **not** can be found between a helping verb and a main verb in a sentence, it is not a verb.

I <u>do</u> **not** <u>want</u> spaghetti for dinner.

The door <u>was</u> **not** <u>closed</u>.

In these sentences, the verbs are **<u>do want</u>** and **<u>was closed</u>**.

The **contraction** form of **not** is never part of the verb phrase, either.

I <u>did</u>**n't** <u>know</u> it would rain.

We <u>are</u>**n't** <u>going</u> to the movies.

In these sentences the verbs are **<u>did know</u>** and **<u>are going</u>**.

More examples (with the verb phrase underlined):
The machine <u>does</u> **not** <u>work</u>.

We <u>have</u>**n't** <u>finished</u> our work.

Peter <u>has</u> **not** <u>done</u> his exercises.

You <u>did</u> **not** <u>have</u> cake for breakfast.

The flowers <u>did**n't** grow</u>.

I <u>do</u> **not** <u>have</u> dirt on my shoes.

She <u>will</u> **not** <u>go</u> to sleep.

Janet <u>does**n't** cook</u> well.

Isabella <u>does</u> **not** <u>speak</u> English.

I <u>will</u> **not** <u>ride</u> my bicycle today.

3.20 Direct Objects

A **direct object** is a noun or a pronoun that comes after the verb and receives the action of the verb. To find the direct object, say the subject and verb followed by **what** or **whom**.

Gary broke the **lamp**.

Eliza taught **Charlotte**.

Gary broke **what**? He broke the **lamp**. **Lamp** is the **direct object** of the first sentence. Eliza taught **whom**? She taught **Charlotte**. **Charlotte** is the **direct object** of the second sentence.

More examples:
John laced his **shoes**. → John laced **what**? **Shoes**.

Philip found **shells**. → Philip found **what**? **Shells**.

Did Lizzie ride a **bike**? → Did Lizzie ride **what**? **Bike**.

The bee stung **me**. → The bee stung **whom**? **Me**.

She opened the **gate**. → She opened **what**? **Gate**.

I called **Tamika**. → I called **whom**? **Tamika**.

Yesterday we saw a **movie**. → We saw **what**? **Movie**.

Omar bought a **shirt**. → Omar bought **what**? **Shirt**.

Mom grounded **me**. → Mom grounded **whom**? **Me**.

The boy threw a **ball**. → The boy threw **what**? **Ball**.

3.21 Diagramming Direct Objects

Each sentence part has its own special place in a diagram. A diagram helps us to understand how the sentence parts work together. To review, here is how the subject and predicate are diagrammed.

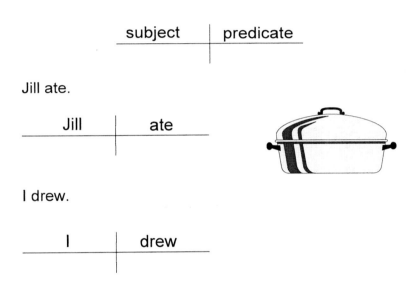

subject | predicate

Jill ate.

Jill | ate

I drew.

I | drew

The subject and predicate are placed on a horizontal line with the subject on the left and the verb on the right. A vertical line separates them.

Here is how a sentence with a **direct object** is diagrammed.

subject | predicate | **direct object**

Jill ate an **apple**.

Jill	ate	apple

I drew a **picture**.

I	drew	picture

The **direct object** is placed on the same line with the subject and predicate. It is separated from the predicate by a short vertical line that doesn't break through the horizontal line.

More examples:

I washed the **dishes**.

I	washed	dishes

Dad cleaned the **garage**.

Dad	cleaned	garage

3.22 No Direct Object

Not every sentence has a **direct object**. If nothing answers the question **whom** or **what**, then there is no direct object.

Colin ran.

The baby cried.

Colin ran **whom** or **what**? The baby cried **whom** or **what**? Nothing answers these questions. These sentences do not have a direct object.

More examples with no direct object:

A bird talks.

The horse jumped.

The lion roared.

Rick spoke.

Johanna giggled.

The telephone rang.

My toe hurts.

We won!

The children play there.

The moth flew away.

Chapter 3 Review

Action Verbs: An **action verb** is a word that tells what the subject is doing. Action verbs can also represent actions that take place but cannot easily be seen.

Verb Tense: -Verbs that show what is happening now are said to be in the **present tense.**
-Verbs that tell about something to happen in the future are called **future tense**.
-Verbs that show what has already happened are called **past tense**.

Forming Past Tense Verbs: -To form the **past tense** of most **verbs**, add **-ed** to the verb.
-Some verbs end with a **consonant letter** and a **y**. Change the **y** to **i** and add **-ed**.
-Some verbs end with a **single vowel** followed by a **single consonant. Double the final consonant** and add **-ed**.

Irregular Verbs: Do **not** add **-ed** to form the past tense of an irregular verb. You must change the spelling of these verbs to form the past tense.

Subject – Verb Agreement: The **subject** and **verb** of a sentence must match.

-If the subject of the sentence is **singular** and means **he, she,** or **it**, use the **-s form** of the verb.

-If the subject of the sentence is **plural** and means **we** or **they**, use the **plain form** of the verb.

Pronoun – Verb Agreement: A **subject pronoun** and its verb must match.

-Use the **-s form** of the verb with the pronouns **he, she,** or **it**.

-If the subject of a sentence is **I, you, we,** or **they**, use the **plain form** of the verb.

Linking Verbs: **Linking verbs** do not show action. They link the subject to a word in the predicate that names or describes it. **Linking verbs** are often forms of the verb **be.**

Using the Forms of Be: -Use **am** or **was** with the pronoun **I**.

-Use **is** or **was** with **she, he, it,** and **singular** nouns.

-Use **are** or **were** with **you, we, they,** and **plural** nouns.

Helping Verbs: A **helping verb** helps another verb. It comes before the main verb to tell about the action.

There are 23 **helping verbs** and they are usually
arranged into five different groups.

-am, is, are, was, were, be, being, been

-have, has, had

-do, does, did

-shall, will, should, would, may, might, must

-can, could

Verb Phrases: A **verb phrase** is a group of words that
has a main verb plus one or more helping verbs. The
main verb is the last word in the verb phrase. The word
not and its contracted form are never part of the verb
phrase.

Do, Does, and Did: When used alone **do**, **does**, and **did**
are **action verbs** and the main verbs in the sentence.

-Use **do** with I, **you**, **we**, **they**, or a **plural subject**.

-Use **does** with **he**, **she**, **it**, or a **singular subject**.

-**Did** is the **past tense** form of the verb **do**.

-When used with another verb, the verb **do** and its forms
does and **did** are **helping verbs**. Use **do**, **does**, or **did**
before the subject when asking a question.

Have, Has, and Had: When used alone, **have**, **has**, and **had** are **action verbs** and the main verbs in the sentence.

-Use **have** with **I**, **you**, **we**, **they**, or a **plural subject**.

-Use **has** with **he**, **she**, **it**, or a **singular subject**.

-**Had** is the **past tense** form of the verb **have**.

-When used with another verb, the verb **have** and its forms **has** and **had** are **helping verbs**. Use **have**, **has**, or **had** before the subject when asking a question.

Contractions: A **contraction** is a single word made by combining two other words. The words are merged and some letters are dropped. The letters that are dropped are replaced by an apostrophe.

Direct Objects: A **direct object** is a noun or a pronoun that comes after the verb and receives the action of the verb. To find the direct object, say the subject and verb followed by **what** or **whom**. Not every sentence has a **direct object**.

Diagramming Direct Objects: The **direct object** is placed on the same line with the subject and predicate. It is separated from the predicate by a short vertical line.

| subject | predicate | **direct object** |

Chapter 4

Growing with Adjectives and Adverbs

4.1 Adjectives That Tell What Kind

An **adjective** is a word that describes a **noun** or a **pronoun**. Adjectives answer the questions **what kind**, **how many**, **which one,** or **whose**.   An adjective usually comes before the noun or the pronoun that it describes.

The first type of adjective answers the question **what kind**. This kind of adjective can explain how things look, smell, sound, feel, or taste.

She wore her **dirty** shoes.

Nathan has **brown** hair.

What kind of shoes? **Dirty**. **What kind** of hair? **Brown**. The words **dirty** and **brown** are adjectives describing the nouns **shoes** and **hair**. They tell **what kind**.

In the following sentences, the **adjectives** that tell **what kind** are in bold.

Lindsay made **delicious** turkey.

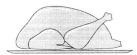

Fat caterpillars eat **juicy green** leaves.

Large trucks make **loud** noises.

Grandma makes **gorgeous square** quilts.

On a sentence diagram, the **adjective** is placed on a slanted line under the noun or pronoun it describes.

Fat caterpillars eat **juicy green** leaves.

caterpillars	eat	leaves

Fat, juicy, green

Cindy wore **fancy blue** slippers.

Cindy	wore	slippers

fancy, blue

4.2 Adjectives That Tell How Many

The second type of **adjective** answers the question **how many**.

There were **nine** children at the party.

I have **several** questions.

How many children? **Nine.** **How many** questions?
Several. The words **nine** and **several** are adjectives
describing the nouns **children** and **questions.** They tell
how many.

Numbers such as **one**, **two**, **four**, and **five** are
adjectives that tell **how many**. Words like **few, many,
some**, and **any** are also adjectives that tell how many.

In the following sentences, the **adjectives** that tell **how
many** are in bold.

We caught **three** fish.

Julia sees **many** squirrels.

There are **numerous** ways to eat potatoes.

My **two** sisters are great swimmers.

Gareth has **several** cousins.

On a sentence diagram, the **adjective** is placed on a slanted line under the noun or pronoun it describes.

We caught **three** fish.

We	caught	fish

three

Julia sees **many** squirrels.

Julia	sees	squirrels

many

4.3 Adjectives That Tell Which One

The third type of adjective answers the question **which one**. The words **this**, **that**, **these,** and **those** are often used to describe **which one** in a sentence.

Those grapes are delicious.

I'll take **this** shirt.

Which grapes? **Those. Which** shirt? **This one.** The words **those** and **this** are used as adjectives describing the nouns **grapes** and **shirt**. They tell **which one**.

This and **these** are used to tell about nouns that are near. **That** and **those** are used to tell about nouns that are far. **This** and **that** are used with singular nouns. **These** and **those** are used with plural nouns.

I love **those** earrings.

William wanted to see **this** movie.

Words such as **first**, **second**, **third**, and **fourth** also tell **which one**.

I was the **third** person in line.

Stacy lives in the **fifth** house.

On a sentence diagram, the **adjective** is placed on a slanted line under the noun or pronoun it describes.

I love **those** earrings.

I	love	earrings

those

Will you eat **these** pears?

you	Will eat	pears

these

4.4 Adjectives That Tell Whose

The fourth type of **adjective** answers the question **whose**. Possessive nouns like **Harry's**, **bird's**, and **boy's** are used as adjectives to tell **whose**. **My, our, your, their, her, his,** and **its** are possessive pronouns that are also used as adjectives to tell **whose**.

Jeremy's dog is sick.

David saw **his** aunt.

Whose dog? **Jeremy's**. **Whose** aunt? **His**. The words **Jeremy's** and **his** are adjectives describing the nouns **dog** and **aunt**. They tell **whose**.

In the following sentences, the **adjectives** that tell **whose** are in bold.

Is that **your** house?

Cody's sister is **my** friend.

Monique lost **her** coat.

I saw a **bird's** nest.

Mrs. Smith is **our** neighbor.

On a sentence diagram, the **adjective** is placed on a slanted line under the noun or pronoun it describes.

Nick's dog ate **my** shoe.

```
dog        | ate    | shoe
  \Nick's  |          \my
```

Jonathan found **his** mouse.

```
Jonathan   | found  | mouse
           |          \his
```

4.5 A, An, and The

Articles are adjectives that announce that a noun is coming. The words **a, an,** and **the** are **articles**. **Articles** are also called **noun markers**.

He gave me **a** banjo.

I ate **an** apple for lunch.

I saw **the** lion at the zoo.

In these sentences, the articles **a, an,** and **the** tell that the nouns **banjo, apple,** and **lion** are coming.

The article **a** is used when a word begins with a consonant. Use **a** with singular nouns.

a pen   **a** baseball   **a** car   **a** door

The words **pen, baseball, car**, and **door** begin with a consonant.

The article **an** is used when a word begins with a vowel. Use **an** with singular nouns.

an apple   **an** exam   **an** oven   **an** umbrella

The words **apple**, **exam**, **oven**, and **umbrella** begin with a vowel.

The article **the** is used when talking about a particular person or thing. Use **the** with singular or plural nouns.

The snake hissed at us.

The cookies were delicious.

The article **the** is used because it refers to the specific nouns **snake** and **cookies**.

Use **the** when talking about a thing that is one of its kind.

The North Pole is very cold.

The Nile River is very long.

In these sentences, **the** is used because there is only one **North Pole** and only one **Nile River**.

4.6 Adjectives Used to Compare

Adjectives can be used to compare two or more different persons or things.

Use the ending **-er** when comparing two things and put the word **than** between the adjective and the thing being compared.

Garrick is **taller than** Arden.

Use the ending **-est** when comparing three or more things.

I have the **darkest** hair in my family.

If the adjective has one syllable, add **-er** or **-est**.

long	long**er**	long**est**
dark	dark**er**	dark**est**
short	short**er**	short**est**

If the adjective ends with an **e**, drop the **e** and add **-er** or **-est**.

large	larg**er**	larg**est**
white	whit**er**	whit**est**
cute	cut**er**	cut**est**

If the one or two syllable adjective ends with a **consonant** and **y**, change the **y** to **i**, then add **-er** or **-est**.

funny	funn**ier**	funn**iest**
pretty	prett**ier**	prett**iest**
happy	happ**ier**	happ**iest**

If the adjective ends with a single consonant after a short vowel, double the final consonant, then add **-er** or **-est**.

big	big**ger**	big**gest**
thin	thin**ner**	thin**nest**
hot	hot**ter**	hot**test**

4.7 Adjectives Used with More and Most

If the adjective has three or more syllables, use **more** or **most** with it. **More** and **most** is also used with some two syllable adjectives.

Joe is **more careful than** Ben.

Erin is the **most likeable** girl I know.

Use **more** to compare two things and put the word **than** between the adjective and the thing being compared. Use **most** to compare three or more things.

beautiful	**more** beautiful	**most** beautiful
harmful	**more** harmful	**most** harmful
pleasant	**more** pleasant	**most** pleasant
delicious	**more** delicious	**most** delicious

However, don't add **-er** to an adjective at the same time you use **more**.

Incorrect: She is more faster than Edward.
Correct: She is **faster** than Edward.

Incorrect: Will is more cheerfuler than Pilar.
Correct: Will is **more cheerful** than Pilar.

Also, don't add **-est** to an adjective at the same time you use **most**.

Incorrect: Al is the most interestingest boy in our family.
Correct: Al is the **most interesting** boy in our family.

Incorrect: That is the most tallest tree in the forest.
Correct: That is the **tallest** tree in the forest.

4.8 Using Bad, Good, Many, and Much

The endings **-er** and **-est** are not added to the adjectives **bad, good, many,** and **much**. Instead, these adjectives change form when they are used to compare.

Lili has **many** books.

Seth has **more** books than Lili.

I have the **most** books of all.

Worse, better, and **more** are used to compare two nouns. **Worst, best,** and **most** are used to compare three or more nouns.

Describing One	Comparing Two	Comparing Three or More
bad	worse	worst
good	better	best
much	more	most
many	more	most

However, don't add **-er** or **-est** to the adjectives **bad, good, many,** and **much**.

Incorrect: The weather is badder than it was yesterday.

Correct: The weather is **worse** than it was yesterday.

Incorrect: Pieter has the muchest medals of all.

Correct: Pieter has the **most** medals of all.

Also, don't use **more** and **most** with the comparing forms of these adjectives.

Incorrect: Your score was more worse than hers.

Correct: Your score was **worse** than hers.

Incorrect: Annelies had the most best time at camp.

Correct: Annelies had the **best** time at camp.

4.9 Writing Sentences with Adjectives

Adjectives answer the questions **what kind**, **how many**, **which one,** or **whose**. **Adjectives** are used to describe and give more detail about the noun. Adding details adds interest and can also make things seem real. To do this, ask the questions that adjectives answer and add the answer to the sentence.

In these examples, details are added to the shorter sentences by using adjectives.

Caterpillars eat leaves.

What kind? Fat caterpillars eat **green** leaves.

How many? Three fat caterpillars eat green leaves.

Which one? Three fat caterpillars eat **those** green leaves.

Whose? Harry's three fat caterpillars eat those green leaves.

Mother gave me earrings.

What kind? Mother gave me **blue** earrings.

How many? Mother gave me **two** blue earrings.

Which one? Mother gave me **those** two blue earrings.

Whose? **My** mother gave me those two blue earrings.

The brothers are swimmers.

What kind? The brothers are **excellent** swimmers.

How many? The **two** brothers are excellent swimmers.

Which one? **Those** two brothers are excellent swimmers.

Whose? **Your** two brothers are excellent swimmers.

4.10 Adverbs That Tell When

Adverbs are words that tell more about verbs. Some adverbs tell **when** something is done.

We saw a bear **today**.

Yesterday I went to the store.

In these sentences, the words **today** and **yesterday** are used as **adverbs** to tell **when** about the verbs **saw** and **went**. Saw **when**? **Today**. Went **when**? **Yesterday**.

Some adverbs that tell when are **tonight, now, tomorrow, then, today, soon, sooner, yesterday, daily, again, first, early, earlier, forever, when, late, later, never, sometimes,** and **always.**

In the following sentences, the **adverbs** that tell **when** are in bold.

Today we will learn about koalas.

Does Joel **usually** lose his glasses?

The recital starts **soon**.

I have **never** seen a starfish.

She **always** changes her mind.

We go to the beach **often**.

The word **when** is also considered an adverb.

When is the movie over?

When is your birthday?

On a sentence diagram, the **adverb** is placed on a slanted line under the verb it describes.

Chantal will sing **later**.

Chantal	will sing

later

When did you eat?

4.11 Adverbs That Tell Where

Some **adverbs** are used with verbs to tell **where** something is done.

Zach played outside.

Mandy lives nearby.

In these sentences, the words **outside** and **nearby** are used as **adverbs** to tell **where** about the verbs **played** and **lives**. Played **where**? **Outside**. Lives **where**? **Nearby**.

Some adverbs that tell **where** are **around, up, down, in, out, inside, where, everywhere, anywhere, somewhere, here, there, away, nowhere, downstairs, and upstairs.**

In the following sentences, the **adverbs** that tell **where** are in bold.

I can't find my pen **anywhere**.

Erick came **in**.

We went **away** for the weekend.

He kicked the ball **far**.

Climb **down** from that tree.

Lucy skipped **everywhere**.

The word **where** is also considered an adverb.

Where did she take the laundry?

Where did you go?

On a sentence diagram, the **adverb** is placed on a slanted line under the verb it describes.

Where is Everett?

Everett | is

Where

Dad ran **downstairs**.

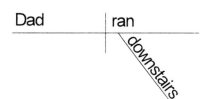

4.12 Adverbs That Tell How

Some **adverbs** are used with verbs to tell **how** something is done.

She danced **gracefully**.

Trevan banged the drum **loudly**.

In these sentences, the words **gracefully** and **loudly** are used as **adverbs** to tell **how** about the verbs **danced** and **banged**. Danced **how**? **Gracefully**. Banged **how**? **Loudly**.

In the following sentences, the **adverbs** that tell **how** are in bold.

She **eagerly** ate her sandwich.

Isabella **quickly** fell asleep.

The children dressed **warmly**.

Keith waited **patiently**.

Jamie walked **slowly**.

She **neatly** packed her suitcase.

The boys played **wildly**.

The word **how** is also considered an adverb.

How did she drive?

How are you feeling?

On a sentence diagram, the **adverb** is placed on a slanted line under the verb it describes.

They fought **bravely**.

How does she sing?

4.13 How to Form Adverbs

Adverbs usually have the ending **-ly**.   Adjectives can often be changed into an adverb by adding **-ly.**

That is a **slow** car.

It moves **slowly.**

Slow is an adjective describing the noun **car**. When the ending **-ly** is added, the word becomes an **adverb**. **Slowly** is an **adverb** telling more about the verb **moves**.

More examples:

proud → proud**ly**   brave → brave**ly**

deep → deep**ly**   quiet → quiet**ly**

clear → clear**ly**   careful → careful**ly**

tight → tight**ly**   quick → quick**ly**

warm → warm**ly**   sad → sad**ly**

Not all adverbs end in **-ly**. There are some exceptions. For example, the words **wrong, late, hard, fast, high, low,** and **right** can be used as adverbs.

I arrived **late**.

She jumped **high**.

George fell **hard**.

Max is running **fast**.

4.14 Using Adverbs to Add Interest

Adverbs answer the questions **when**, **where**, or **how**. Adverbs are used to give detail about the verb. Adding details builds sentences and adds interest. To do this, ask the questions that adverbs answer and add the answer to the sentence.

In these examples, details are added to the original, short sentences by using adverbs.

I take the laundry.

Where?   I take the laundry **upstairs**.
How?   I take the laundry upstairs **quickly**.
When?   **Usually** I take the laundry upstairs quickly.

Lucy skips.

Where?   Lucy skips **everywhere**.
How?   Lucy skips **happily** everywhere.
When?   Lucy **always** skips happily everywhere.

Kylan waits.

Where?   Kylan waits **here**.

How?   Kylan waits here **patiently**.

When?   Kylan **usually** waits here patiently.

The children played.

How?   The children played **quietly**.

Where?   The children played quietly **downstairs**.

When?   **Today** the children played quietly downstairs.

4.15 Negative Words

A **negative word** is a word that means **no** or **not**. The words **no, not, none, nothing, nowhere, neither, nobody, no one,** and **never** are considered negative words. If you use them in your sentences once, your statements will be negative.

One negative word in a sentence is enough. In fact, when two negative words are used in one sentence it is called a **double negative**, which makes the meaning of a sentence unclear, or incorrect, and should not be used.

Incorrect: I **don't** want **no** carrots.

Correct: I **don't** want any carrots.

Correct: I want **no** carrots.

In the incorrect sentence, both **don't** and **no** are **negatives**. **Don't** is the contraction for **do not**. Some other negative contractions are **doesn't, can't, aren't, hasn't, and isn't**.

Incorrect: Grant **can't** go **nowhere**.

Correct: Grant **can't** go anywhere.

Correct: Grant can go **nowhere**.

Incorrect: Eva **hasn't** had **nothing** to eat.

Correct: Eva **hasn't** had anything to eat.

Correct: Eva has had **nothing** to eat.

Incorrect: The boy **didn't** like **none**.

Correct: The boy **didn't** like any.

Correct: The boy liked **none**.

Incorrect: There **aren't no** seats left.

Correct: There **aren't** any seats left.

Correct: There are **no** seats left.

Some negative words are adverbs. On a sentence diagram, a negative word that is used as an adverb is placed on a slanted line under the verb it describes.

She had **not** eaten.

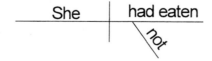

4.16 Synonyms

Synonyms are words that have the same or almost the same meaning.

small   little

The words **small** and **little** are **synonyms**. Either one could be used in the same sentence.

The mouse is **small.**

The mouse is **little**.

Both sentences have the same meaning.

More examples:

The stick is **crooked**. → The stick is **bent**.

The towel is still **damp**. → The towel is still **wet**.

I ate a **big** bite of melon. → I ate a **huge** bite of melon.

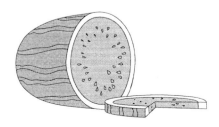

My birthday is this **autumn**. → My birthday is this **fall**.

That **woman** is my mother. → That **lady** is my mother.

Tony **talked** to his father. → Tony **spoke** to his father.

Can we **go** now? → Can we **leave** now?

We love to skip **rocks**. → We love to skip **stones**.

I live in a brick **house**. → I live in a brick **home**.

Did you **shut** the door? → Did you **close** the door?

4.17 Antonyms

Antonyms are words with opposite meanings.

night   day

The words **night** and **day** are **antonyms**. **Night** is the opposite of **day**.

More examples:

hard / soft   pull / push

empty / full   start / stop

laugh / cry   long / short

give / take   good / bad

long / short   beginning / end

up / down   early / late

lost / found   whisper / shout

walk / run   inside / outside

same / different   awake / asleep

dark / light   clean / dirty

4.18 Homonyms

Homonyms are words with the same sound, but they have different spellings and meanings.

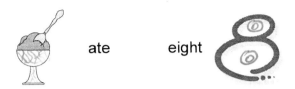

ate   eight

The words **ate** and **eight** are **homonyms**. Although they sound the same, they have different meanings and often are different parts of speech.

We **ate** pizza.

I am **eight** years old.

The bold words in these two sentences do not have the same meaning.

More examples:

I **won** the race. → There was only **one** winner.

The **ant** crawled on my toe. → My **Aunt** Nell is visiting.

I want to **be** a scientist. → Did that **bee** sting you?

I love the **scent** of roses. → Mom **sent** me to the store.

There is **dew** on the grass. → **Do** you want stay?

The birds **flew** across the sky. → I think I have the **flu**.

Did you **write** a letter? → Do you use your **right** hand?

Please put the book **here**. → Did you **hear** what I said?

The wind **blew**. → The water was **blue**.

Did you **close** the door? → Did you buy new **clothes**?

4.19 Friendly Letters

A **friendly letter** is a letter that is usually written to a friend and often contains information about you. It also may ask questions about the friend to whom you are writing. There are five parts to a friendly letter.

The first part is the **heading**. The heading is in the upper right corner of the letter and contains your address and the date.

Example: 123 Main Street
                        Chicago, IL 60601
                        July 1, 20-

The second part is the **greeting.**

Example: Dear Anthony,

The third part is the **body** of the letter. This part includes all of the information and questions for the person to whom you are writing. Each paragraph should be indented.

The fourth part is the **closing,** and the fifth part is your name or **signature** after the closing.

Example: Yours truly,

                      Jeremy

This is what the entire letter would look like:

(Heading)	123 Main Street
	Chicago, IL 60601
	July 1, 20-

(Greeting)   Dear Anthony,

(Body)   --

(Closing)   Yours truly,

(Signature)   Jeremy

4.20 Thank You Letters

A **thank you letter** is written to show appreciation for something that someone has done for you or given to you. A thank you letter should be written soon after the thoughtful act.

If a gift was received, then mention what the gift was and tell why you appreciate it.

Dear Grandma,

Thank you so much for the beautiful watch you gave me. I have wanted it for a long time. I put the watch on after I opened it, and I haven't taken it off since.

With love,

Isabella

If something kind was done for you, then you should also send a prompt thank you note mentioning the kind act and why you appreciate it.

Dear Tim,

I wanted to let you know how much I appreciate you mowing my lawn while I was ill. It was very kind of you to do this for me since I was unable to. You are very thoughtful.

Sincerely,

Uncle Edward

4.21 Capitalizing and Punctuating in Letters

There are specific rules for capitalization and punctuation in letters.

In the **heading**, make sure to capitalize all proper nouns. This would include the names of all months, cities, states, and provinces. Use commas correctly in the heading. Put a comma between the city and state in an address. Put a comma between the day's date and the year in the date.

> 123 **Main Street**
> **Chicago, IL** 60601
> **July** 1, 20-

In the **greeting**, be sure to capitalize the first word of the greeting and any other word if it is a name or title. Put a comma after the greeting.

Dear Anthony,   Dear Mrs. Smith,

My dear friend,   Dear Dr. Charles,

In the **closing**, be sure to capitalize the first word, and put a comma after the closing.

Yours truly,   Sincerely,

With love,   Your aunt,

The **signature** is your name and should be capitalized.

4.22 How to Address an Envelope

After you have finished writing your letter you will need to mail it. However, before the letter is mailed you will need to address an envelope so the letter arrives at the correct address.

The **first step** is to write your own name and address in the upper left-hand corner of the envelope. This is called the **return address** and tells who is sending the letter.

The **second step** is to write your friend's name and address in the center of the envelope. This is called the **mailing address** and tells where and to whom the letter is being sent.

The **last step** is to put a stamp in the upper right hand corner. Your letter is now ready to be mailed.

Lillian Jones
20 Star Drive
Los Angeles CA 90065

36¢

Jane Smith
123 Elm Lane
Omaha NE 68122

Chapter 4 Review

Adjectives: An **adjective** is a word that describes a **noun** or a **pronoun**. Adjectives answer the questions **what kind**, **how many**, **which one**, or **whose**.   An adjective usually comes before the noun or the pronoun that it describes.   **Adjectives** can also be used to compare two or more different persons or things.

On a sentence diagram, the **adjective** is placed on a slanted line under the noun or pronoun it describes.

Fat caterpillars eat **juicy green** leaves.

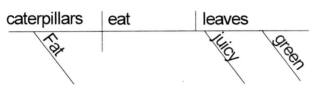

Articles: The words **a, an,** and **the** are adjectives that tell that a noun is coming. They are called **noun markers**.

Using Bad, Good, Many, and Much: The endings **-er** and **-est** are not added to the adjectives **bad, good, many,** and **much**. These adjectives change form when they are used to compare. **Worse, better,** and **more** are used to compare two nouns. **Worst, best,** and **most** are used to compare three or more nouns.

-Don't add **-er** or **-est** to the adjectives **bad, good, more,** and **most**. Don't use **more** and **most** with the comparing forms of these adjectives

Adverbs: **Adverbs** are words that tell more about verbs. Some **adverbs** are used with verbs to tell **when, where,** or **how** something is done.

-**Adverbs** usually have the ending **ly**. Adjectives can often be changed into an adverb by adding **-ly.**

-Not all adverbs end in **ly**. The words **wrong, late, hard, fast, high, low,** and **right** can be used as adverbs.

On a sentence diagram, the **adverb** is placed on a slanted line under the verb it describes.

Mom stopped **suddenly**.

Negative Words: A **negative word** is an adverb that means **no** or **not**. When two negative words are used in one sentence it is called a **double negative,** which makes the meaning of a sentence unclear and should not be used.

On a sentence diagram, a **negative word** is placed on a slanted line under the verb it describes.

She had **not** eaten.

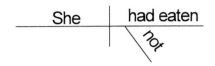

Synonyms: **Synonyms** are words that have the same or almost the same meaning.

Antonyms: **Antonyms** are words with opposite meanings**.**

Homonyms: **Homonyms** are words with the same sound, but with different spellings and meanings.

Friendly Letters: There are **five** parts to a friendly letter.
-The first part is the **heading**
-The second part is the **greeting**
-The third part is the **body** of the letter.
-The fourth part is the **closing.**
-The fifth part is your name or **signature** after the closing.

Thank-you Letter: A **thank-you letter** is written to show appreciation for something that someone has done for you or given to you.

How to Address an Envelope: The **first step** is to write your own name and address in the upper left-hand corner of the envelope.   The **second step** is to write your friend's name and address in the center of the envelope. The **last step** is to put a stamp in the upper right-hand corner.

Chapter 5

Growing with Words and Punctuation

5.1 Can or May

Use the word **can** to show or ask if someone has the ability or is capable of doing something.

Lucy can swim.

Can Johanna speak French?

In the first sentence, the word **can** is being used to show that Lucy has the ability to swim. In the second sentence, the word **can** is being used to ask if Johanna has the ability to speak French.

More examples:

Can Everett hit a home run?

I **can** run faster than my brother.

Do you think I **can** lift this rock?

Julie **can** write beautiful poems.

Can you do a back flip?

Use the word **may** to ask or give permission to do something.

You **may** borrow my sweater.

May we go outside?

In the first sentence, the word **may** is being used to give permission to borrow a sweater. In the second sentence, the word **may** is being used to ask permission to go outside.

More examples:

May I have ice cream?

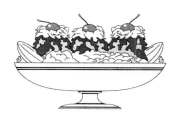

You **may** ride your bike.

May I watch television?

Amy **may** take a walk now.

May I go to the soccer game?

5.2 Who's or Whose

It is easy to confuse **who's** and **whose**. The words sound alike but are spelled differently and have different meanings.

Who's is a contraction that means **who is** or **who has.**

Who is next in line? → **Who's** next in line?

Who has taken my gum? → **Who's** taken my gum?

More examples:

Who's been knocking on the door?

I know **who's** been eating my candy.

Who's going to the movies with me?

Who's playing in the game today?

Annelies knows **who's** at home.

Whose is a possessive pronoun and shows ownership.
Use **whose** to mean **something belonging to someone**.

Whose bunny is this?

Whose book was lost?

Whose house did they visit?

I know **whose** bicycle this is.

Whose bed were you jumping on?

Whose toy are you playing with?

Do you know **whose** mess this is?

Try replacing **who's** with **who is** or **who has** in the
sentence. If **who is** or **who has** does not sound right in
the sentence, then use **whose**.

5.3 Abbreviations

Abbreviations are short ways to write a word. Most abbreviations begin with a capital letter and end with a period.

The names of the **days of the week** can be abbreviated. They are capitalized and followed by a period.

Sunday → Sun.	Monday → Mon.
Tuesday → Tues.	Wednesday → Wed.
Thursday → Thurs.	Friday → Fri.
Saturday → Sat.	

Most of the names of the **months** of the year can be abbreviated. They are capitalized and followed by a period. May, June, and July are usually not abbreviated.

January → Jan.	February → Feb.
March → Mar.	April → Apr.
August → Aug.	September → Sept.
October → Oct.	November → Nov.
December → Dec.	

The names of the **50 states, territories, and Canadian provinces** are also abbreviated. Two initials are used with no period.

Arizona → AZ   Georgia → GA   Oregon → OR

Maryland → MD   Nevada → NV   New York → NY

District of Columbia→ DC   Quebec → QC

Names can be abbreviated. These abbreviations are called **initials**. The initial can be used for the first name, middle name, or all parts of a name. Initials are capitalized and followed by a period.

Ari Patel → A. Patel   Eli John Cook→ E.J. Cook

Lia Ann Lyle → L.A.L.   Joe Lee Neil → Joe L. Neil

Titles before and after names are also abbreviated. They are capitalized and followed by a period. **Miss** is a title that is not abbreviated.

Mister → Mr.   Mistress → Mrs.   Doctor → Dr.

Junior → Jr.   Senior → Sr.

Names of **streets** have abbreviations too. They are capitalized and followed by a period.

Street → St.   Avenue → Ave.   Road → Rd.

Drive → Dr.   Lane → Ln.   Court → Ct.

5.4 Set or Sit

Use the word **set** to mean **to put** or **place something in a special or certain position**.

Set the peaches on the table.

I **set** the cake on the counter.

Set requires a direct object. In these sentences, **peaches** and **cake** are the objects for the action **set**. What did you **set** on the table? The **peaches**. What did you **set** on the counter? The **cake**.

More examples:

Have you **set** the clock to go off at three?

She **sets** her bag on the desk.

Set the boxes on the floor.

My sister loves **setting** the table.

Where should we **set** the statue?

Use the word **sit** to mean **to be seated** or **to rest**.

Please **sit** on the couch.

We usually **sit** at the table to play cards.

Sit does not require a direct object. What did you **sit**?
Nothing. The words after **sit** tell where.

More examples:

Do you think we should **sit** there?

Jennifer likes **sitting** in the front row.

May I **sit** here?

How long has she been **sitting** there?

The puppy loves to **sit** in front of the fireplace.

5.5   Gone and Went

Gone is a past form of the verb **go**. Used as the verb of a sentence, **go** must always be used with a helping verb.

Incorrect: He **gone** to the game.
Correct: He **has gone** to the game.

Incorrect: I **gone** to ballet.
Correct: I **have gone** to ballet.

More examples:

Incorrect: We **gone** to the store.
Correct: We **have gone** to the store.

Incorrect: Ella **gone** with Flora.
Correct: Ella **had gone** with Flora.

Incorrect: Diego **gone** to Victor's house.
Correct: Diego **has gone** to Victor's house.

Incorrect: Alyson and Bradyn **gone** to sleep.
Correct: Alyson and Bradyn **have gone** to sleep.

Went is also a past form of **go**. It is never used with a helping verb.

Incorrect: They **have went** to the movies.
Correct: They **went** to the movies.

Incorrect: I **have went** shopping.
Correct: I **went** shopping.

More examples:

Incorrect: We **had went** to dinner.
Correct: We **went** to dinner.

Incorrect: Margaret **has went** to Grandma's house.
Correct: Margaret **went** to Grandma's house.

Incorrect: I **have went** there yesterday.
Correct: I **went** there yesterday.

Incorrect: They **had went** to the party.
Correct: They **went** to the party.

5.6 You're or Your

You're and **your** are words that sound alike, but they are spelled differently and have different meanings.

You're is a contraction that means **you are**.

You are very tall. → **You're** very tall.

You are beautiful. → **You're** beautiful.

More examples:

You're going to have a great time.

You're the best friend I have.

Are you sure **you're** okay?

I'm not sure what **you're** talking about.

We can leave when **you're** ready.

Your is a possessive pronoun and shows ownership. Use **your** to mean **belonging to you.**

The car **belonging to you** is fast. → **Your** car is fast.

The hat **belonging to you** is blue. → **Your** hat is blue.

More examples:

Your key fell on the floor.

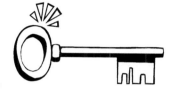

What is **your** telephone number?

Is that **your** necklace?

What is **your** favorite song?

Did you lose **your** tooth?

Try replacing **you're** with **you are** in the sentence. If **you are** does not sound right, then use **your**.

5.7 The Apostrophe

One of the reasons we use **apostrophes** is to show possession. Possession means that a person or living thing has or owns something.

the dress of the girl → the girl's dress

the idea of the boy → the boy's idea

More examples:

Dad's books   Dora's toy
the cat's whiskers   Charlotte's piano
the lion's paw   Todd's dream

Another reason we use **apostrophes** is to show where a letter is dropped in a **contraction**. A contraction is a single word made by combining two other words. The words are merged and some letters are dropped.

Examples:

I am → I'm   I would → I'd

you will → you'll   you are → you're

he would → he'd   he is → he's

she is → she's   she would → she'd

it is → it's   it will → it'll

we are → we're   we have → we've

they would → they'd   they will → they'll

who is → who's   who would → who'd

that is → that's   that will → that'll

are not → aren't   does not → doesn't

should not → shouldn't   let us → let's

there is → there's   there have →there've

what is → what's   who is → who's

5.8 Lay or Lie

Use the word **lay** to mean **to put** or **place something somewhere**.

Hens **lay** eggs.

Lay the flowers on the counter.

Lay requires a direct object. In these sentences, **eggs** and **flowers** are the objects for the action **lay**. What do hens **lay**? **Eggs**. What did you **lay** on the counter? The **flowers**.

More examples:

Did you **lay** the papers on the desk?

Please **lay** the clothes on the chair.

Lay the baby on the bed.

When will they **lay** the new carpet?

Dad **lays** his keys on the table when he comes home.

Use the word **lie** to mean **to rest** or **recline**.

Lie back and relax.

I like to **lie** in the hammock.

Lie does not require a direct object. What did you **lie**? Nothing. The words after **lie** tell where.

More examples:

If you are sick, you should **lie** down.

Our house **lies** on a small piece of land.

Are you going to **lie** on the floor to watch television?

The cat **lies** on the couch to sleep.

I will **lie** down for a nap.

5.9 Good or Well

Good and **well** are often used incorrectly. **Good** is an adjective that answers the question **what kind of**. Never use it after an action verb. Use **good** to describe nouns.

This is a **good** song.

You did a **good** job.

In the first sentence, **good** describes **what kind** of song. In the second sentence, **good** describes **what kind** of job.

More examples:

Jacob is a **good** basketball player.

Dad made a **good** lunch for us.

I am having a **good** day.

Well is an adverb that tells **how** something is done. Use **well** after an action verb.

The hat fits Sarah **well**.

Elliot did **well** on the test.

In the first sentence, **well** describes **how** the hat fit. In the second sentence, **well** describes **how** Elliot did on the test.

More examples:

The band played **well**.

The cat climbed the tree **well**.

I did **well** on the test.

Well is also used to mean **not sick**.

Earlier my brother was very sick, but now he is **well**.

Are you feeling **well**?

You do not look **well** today.

5.10 It's or Its

It's and its are two words that sound alike, but they are spelled differently and have different meanings.

It's is a contraction that means it is or it has.

It is an exciting game. → It's an exciting game.

It has been a beautiful day. → It's been a beautiful day.

More examples:

Did you know it's snowing?

It's too late to catch the bus.

It's my turn to water the plants.

Are you sure it's time to leave?

It's been raining for a week.

Its is a possessive pronoun and shows ownership. Use **its** to mean **belonging to it.**

The tail **belonging to it** was red. → **Its** tail was red.

The leg **belonging to it** was hurt. → **Its** leg was hurt.

More examples:

The river is at **its** lowest point.

The dog stopped **its** barking.

Has the cat had **its** bath?

The tree has lost **its** leaves.

The lion lifted **its** head quickly.

Try replacing **it's** with **it is** or **it has** in the sentence. If **it is** or **it has** does not sound right in the sentence, then use **its**.

5.11 Capital Letters

Capitalize the **first letter** of the first word in a **sentence**.

The dog chased its tail.
She laughed so hard she fell off the couch.

Capitalize the **first word** of a **direct quote**.

Toby said, "Where are you going?"
"They lost the game," said Greg.

Capitalize the **first word** in a line of **poetry**.

Roses are red,
  Violets are blue.
I'm feeling great,
  How about you?

Capitalize the **first word** of a **greeting** in a letter

Dear Uncle Vernon,
Dear Mr. President,

Capitalize the **first word** of a **closing** in a letter

Sincerely,
Your friend,

Capitalize the **first word**, **last word**, and all **important words** in **titles**. Do not capitalize a, an, the, and, but, or small words unless they are the first or last word in a title.

Growing With Grammar
The Hobbit
The Tortoise and the Hare

Begin the **first word** and every other important word in a **proper noun** with a capital letter.

Australia
Mr. Abraham J. Baker
Friday
Labor Day
Metropolitan Museum of Art

5.12 Done and Did

Done is a past form of the verb **do**. It should not be used alone as the verb of a sentence. **Done** should always follow a **helping verb**.

Incorrect: He **done** a craft.
Correct: He has **done** a craft.

Incorrect: You **done** well.
Correct: You **have done** well.

More examples:

Incorrect: I **done** what I was supposed to do.
Correct: I **have done** what I was supposed to do.

Incorrect: Spencer **done** his shopping.
Correct: Spencer **has done** his shopping.

Incorrect: You **done** the laundry.
Correct: You **had done** the laundry.

Did is also a past form of **do**. Never use a helping verb with **did.**

Incorrect: He **has did** a craft.

Correct: He **did** a craft.

Incorrect: You **have did** well.

Correct: You **did** well.

More examples:

Incorrect: We **had did** nothing wrong.

Correct: We **did** nothing wrong.

Incorrect: She **had did** something nice.

Correct: She **did** something nice.

Incorrect: You **had did** all of the cooking.

Correct: You **did** all of the cooking.

5.13 Seen and Saw

Seen is a past form of the verb **see**. It must always be used with a helping verb.

Incorrect: I **seen** it.
Correct: I **have seen** it.

Incorrect: She **seen** the movie.
Correct: She **has seen** the movie.

More examples:

Incorrect: We **seen** all of them.
Correct: We **have seen** all of them.

Incorrect: Bart **seen** the new neighbor.
Correct: Bart **has seen** the new neighbor.

Incorrect: I **seen** William at the park.
Correct: I **had seen** William at the park.

Incorrect: They **seen** some strange things.
Correct: They **have seen** some strange things.

Saw is also a past form of **see**. No helping verb is used with **saw.**

Incorrect: We **have saw** three deer.

Correct: We **saw** three deer.

Incorrect: I **had saw** the fireworks.

Correct: I **saw** the fireworks.

More examples:

Incorrect: They **had saw** the Grand Canyon.

Correct: They **saw** the Grand Canyon.

Incorrect: Victoria **has saw** us crossing the street.

Correct: Victoria **saw** us crossing the street.

Incorrect: I **have saw** my friend at the store.

Correct: I **saw** my friend at the store.

Incorrect: Dion **had saw** a butterfly in the yard.

Correct: Dion **saw** a butterfly in the yard.

5.14 Using They're, Their, and There

They're, their, and **there** are words that sound alike but are spelled differently and have different meanings.

They're is a contraction that means **they are**.

They are studying. → **They're** studying.

More examples:

They're at the birthday party.

They're being very quiet.

They're not going to the movie with us.

Do the girls know where **they're** going?

Their is a possessive pronoun and shows ownership. Use **their** to mean **belonging to them.**

A car **belonging to them** is red. → **Their** car is red.

More examples:

I hope **their** team wins the race.

The boys gave **their** opinions.

Their voices are very loud.

Where are **their** coats?

There is a word that is often used at the beginning of a sentence. **There** also tells where.

There is a hole in my mitten.

We went **there** yesterday.

More examples:

There are two days left of our vacation.

There are no more cookies left.

I want to go **there**.

They went **there** in November.

5.15 Prefixes

A **prefix** is a letter or group of letters added to the beginning of a word to make a new word.

in + complete = **in**complete   in + habit = **in**habit

The prefix **in-** means **not** or **within**.   In the first example, the word **incomplete** means **not complete**. In the second example, the word **inhabit** means **to live within**.

More examples:

indirect = not direct   **in**visible = not visible

incorrect = not correct   **in**expensive= not expensive

Every prefix has a meaning. There are many prefixes. Three of them are **mis-, -re-,** and **un-**.

The prefix **mis-** means **wrong** or **incorrect**.

misjudge = judge incorrectly   **mis**treat = treat incorrectly

misbehave = behave wrongly   **mis**read = read wrongly

The prefix **re-** means **back** or **again**.

renew = new again   **re**charge = charge again

review = view again   **re**arrange = arrange again

The prefix **un-** means **not** or **the opposite of**.

unhappy = not happy   **un**kind = not kind

unsafe = not safe   **un**salted = not salted

5.16 Using Commas

Use a comma to separate **three or more items** in a series.   These items can either be words or phrases. The number of commas that should be used in a series is **one fewer than the number of items**. If you have three items, you should use two commas. If you have four items, you should use three commas.

Garrick found frogs, lizards, and snakes at the pond.

The kids went swimming, played, and took a nap.

Mandy, Eliza, Arden, and Charlotte are good friends.

We sang, played, and watched cartoons at my house.

Cows, pigs, sheep, and horses are all mammals.

We had pizza, salad, and bread for dinner.

Use a comma before **and** or **but** in a compound sentence. A compound sentence is two or more simple sentences joined by words like **and** or **but**.

My dad loves to cook, and my mom loves to eat.

I'm going to Kate's house, but I have to clean first.

Mom folded the clothes, but I put them away.

I planted red flowers, but Andy planted a tree.

Robin loves to sing, and Suzanne plays the piano.

The cat purred, and the dog wagged its tail.

5.17 More Rules for Commas

Use a comma after **yes**, **no**, or **well** at the beginning of a sentence.

No, I didn't have lunch yet.

Yes, you may play in the snow.

Well, are the tomatoes rotten?

Yes, we are going to the library.

No, Janell did not break the vase.

Well, was he faster than you?

Use a comma with **nouns of direct address**. A noun of direct address is the name of the person to whom you are speaking.

Ken and Lisa, come over here.

Have you seen my hat, Mike?

Troy and Jason, please clean the bathroom.

I hurt my toe, Mom.

Will, is that your turtle?

Sami, choose a book to read.

5.18 Using Commas in Addresses, Dates, and Letters

As we have discussed before, there are specific rules for **commas** when used in **addresses** and **dates**.

Place a comma between a **city** and **state**, **province**, or **country**.

Little Rock, Arkansas   Gilbert, Arizona

Halifax, Nova Scotia   Paris, France

Place a comma between the **day** and **year** in a date.

October 2, 1964   September 30, 1997

April 8, 2000   January 25, 1942

There are specific rules for **commas** used in **letters**.
Use a comma after the **greeting** in a friendly letter.

Dear Marie,   Dear Mrs. Moore,

My dear friend,   Dear Dr. Avery,

Use a comma after the **closing** in a friendly letter.

Sincerely,   Yours truly,

Best regards,   Your friend,

Chapter 5 Review

Can or May: Use the word **can** to show that someone has the ability or is capable of doing something. Use the word **may** to ask or give permission to do something.

Who's or Whose: **Who's** is a contraction that means **who is** or **who has**. **Whose** is a possessive pronoun and shows ownership. Use **whose** to mean **something belonging to someone**.

Abbreviations: **Abbreviations** are short ways to write a word. Most abbreviations begin with a capital letter and end with a period.
-The names of the **days of the week** are abbreviated.
-Most of the names of the **months** of the year can be abbreviated.
-The names of the **fifty states, territories, and Canadian provinces** can be abbreviated.
-**Names** can be abbreviated. These abbreviations are called **initials**.
-**Titles** before and after names can be abbreviated.
-Names of **streets** can be abbreviated.

Set or Sit: Use the word **set** to mean to put or place something in a special or certain position. Use the word **sit** to mean **to be seated** or **to rest**.

Gone and Went: **Gone** and **Went** are past forms of the verb **go**. Used as the verb of a sentence, **gone** must always be used with a helping verb. **Went** is never used with a helping verb.

You're or Your: **You're** is a contraction that means **you are**. **Your** is a possessive pronoun and shows ownership. Use **your** to mean **belonging to you.**

The Apostrophe: One of the reasons we use **apostrophes** is to show possession. Another is to show where a letter is dropped in a **contraction**.

Lay or Lie: Use the word **lay** to mean **to put** or **place something somewhere**. Use the word **lie** to mean **to rest** or **recline**.

Good or Well: **Good** is an adjective that answers the question **what kind of**. Never use it after an action verb. Use **good** to describe nouns. **Well** is an adverb that tells **how** something is done. Use **well** to describe verbs, adjectives, and other adverbs. **Well** is also used to mean **not sick.**

It's or Its: **It's** is a contraction that means **it is** or **it has.** **Its** is a possessive pronoun and shows ownership. Use **its** to mean **belonging to it.**

Capital Letters: -Capitalize the first letter of the first word in a **sentence.**
-Capitalize the first word of a **direct quote.**
-Capitalize the first word in a line of **poetry.**
-Capitalize the first word of a **greeting** in a letter.
-Capitalize the first word of a **closing** in a letter.
-Capitalize the first word, last word, and all important words in **titles.** Do not capitalize a, an, the, and, but, or small unimportant words unless they are the first or last word.
-Begin the first word and every other important word in a **proper noun** with a capital letter.

Done and Did: **Done** is a past form of the verb **do.** It should not be used alone as the verb of a sentence. **Done** should always follow a **helping verb**. **Did** is also a past form of **do.** Never use a helping verb with **did.**

Seen and Saw: **Seen** is a past form of the verb **see.** It must always be used with a helping verb. **Saw** is also a past form of **see.** No helping verb is used with **saw.**

Using They're, Their, and There: **They're** is a contraction that means **they are**. **Their** is a possessive pronoun that shows ownership. Use **their** to mean **belonging to them**. **There** is a word that is often used at the beginning of a sentence. **There** also tells where.

Prefixes: A **prefix** is a letter or group of letters added to the beginning of a word to make a new word.
-The prefix **in-** means **not** or **within**.
-The prefix **mis-** means **wrong** or **incorrect**.
-The prefix **re-** means **back** or **again**.
-The prefix **un-** means **not** or **the opposite of**.

Using Commas: -Use a comma to separate **three or more items** in a series.
-Use a comma before **and** or **but** in a compound sentence.
-Use a comma after **yes**, **no**, or **well** at the beginning of a sentence.
-Use a comma with **nouns of direct address**.
-Use a comma between a **city** and **state**, **province**, or **country**.
-Use a comma between the **day** and **year** in a date.
-Use a comma after the **greeting** in a friendly letter.
-Use a comma after the **closing** in a friendly letter.

<<This page intentionally left blank>>